Till Death Do Us Part?

By
Joseph A. Webb

Published by
WEBB MINISTRIES, INC.
P.O. Box 520729
Longwood, Florida 32752-0729

Till Death Do Us Part?

Quote from **Christianity Today**, "Homosexuality: Biblical Guidance Through a Moral Morass", Copyright April 18, 1980, Carol Stream, IL 60188. Used by permission.

Quote from Smith, Preserved, **Erasmus, a Study of His Life, Ideals, and Place in History** New York: Copyright 1962, Frederick Unger Publishing. Used by permission.

Quotes from Albert Barnes' **Barnes on the New Testament**, Copyright 1954, Baker Publishing Co., Ada, Michigan. Used by permission.

Quotes from W. E. Vine's **Vines' Expository Dictionary of Old and New Testament Words**, Copyright 1981; Baker Publishing Co., Ada, Michigan: Used by permission.

ISBN 0-9632226-2-7

Dedication

I wish to dedicate this book to my family.

First, I dedicate this book to my Lord Jesus Christ who redeemed my life from death and destruction on June 13, 1951, and has never failed me.

Secondly, to my wife of two years, Patricia, who came into my life after I had been a widower for over eight years and has brought me joy and been a constant helpmeet in all areas of ministry. She has continuously encouraged me during difficult times and supported me in this arduous work. How I thank the Lord for her.

Thirdly, I dedicate this book to my daughter and son, Jodi and Jeffrey. Their prayers and encouragements, steadfast zeal for Christ, and applied talents, helping to prepare this book, were the greatest confirmations to me, that I experienced in my home, the very family life that God desires everyone to have. Jeffrey went to be with the Lord in January of 1989 at the age of 26.

Acknowledgements

The time-consuming work of rewriting a book can only be appreciated by those who have experienced it.

The value of having competent help is beyond measure.

My wife, Patricia, has patiently, yet diligently urged me to complete this difficult task and manifested her organizational ability in helping me to restructure its contents in a more orderly progression.

Mrs. Rose Brooke and Mrs. Christy King, truly came to our rescue with their invaluable computer expertise and patience to see this task to its completion. It is they who are responsible for the excellent appearance of the book's contents.

Additional help through reading and editing of these pages was graciously given by a dear friend, Mr. Ed Ware.

The book cover was designed by professional artist, Edward French.

There are some subtle messages hidden by the artist in the cover's design that the average onlooker might miss. Did you notice the question mark (?) after the title line? This was to emphasize that most people today are speaking these words of **fact** as a question. The fingers on the hands are crossed, expressing the hopeful attitude of many newlyweds today, **hoping** their marriage will last.

I thank God for the committed talents of these people.

Joseph A. Webb

Foreword

TILL DEATH DO US PART? is not, and from its inception, was not intended to be another **"me too"** book addressing the subjects of marriage and divorce. If one is seeking a book that gives today's **common** answers on these subjects, let him be warned that this is **not** such a book.

This book shares with you **not** a **new truth**, but an **old truth** which God has revealed to me after years of intense study.

This book will be appreciated by those whose first loyalty is to the Word of God, rather than traditions and doctrines of men, who are willing to weigh the evidence and rethink popular opinions. It will expose **the true source** of most of the current teachings being offered through the Christian media of our land. It will **always** be at variance with the opinions and views of *"the world,"* and **often** with today's teachings on marriage and divorce by many fundamental, evangelical, and holiness brethren.

I greatly value and respect the "right" of these other men to preach and teach what they believe. Concerning the subjects of marriage and divorce however, in many cases, I have found that I cannot respect **what** they are saying.

My only request is that those who read these pages **respect my right to be heard,** and judge what I present only in the light of consistent Biblical hermeneutics.

I do not claim this book to be anything near an exhaustive thesis. It is, however, a sufficient study showing the true teachings of the early church, and how these teachings were corrupted. It is written for those desiring a non-contradictive, consistent approach from the Word, concerning marriage and divorce.

This generation, like none before it, is witnessing the *"leaven"* of humanistic philosophy that has permeated the church, and is corrupting earlier fundamental, evangelical, and holiness theology. This subtle permeation has come cloaked in the false guise of compassion, grace and mercy, and has affected the teaching principles of many men of God, who in other areas of doctrine display an outstanding ability to *"rightly divide the Word of Truth."* These men, make no mistake about it, love our Lord deeply. They are preaching and teaching their messages in deepest sincerity and compassion, attempting to comfort those snared and hurting.

The conclusions reached in this book may disturb many; but know this: It is kinder to disturb with truth, than to comfort someone with solutions based upon false premises, to their own hurt.

In the book of Acts, Jesus Christ described to Paul the Apostle the type of ministry to which Paul would be called.

Acts 26:18 (Living Bible)
*"To open their eyes to their **true condition** so that they may **repent** and live in the light of God, instead of in Satan's darkness, **so that** they may receive forgiveness for their sins, and God's inheritance along with all people everywhere whose sins are cleansed away, who are set apart by faith in me."*

Joseph Webb

Preface

"I Joseph, take thee Patricia, to be my lawfully wedded wife...to have and to hold from this day forth, and do promise (or vow) **before God** and these witnesses, to love, honor, protect, and keep you, for better or for worse, for richer or for poorer, in sickness and in health; and to cleave to you, and you only **TILL DEATH DO US PART,** or for as long as we both shall live."

Sound familiar? Certainly not verbatim, but this vow basically represents what we recognize as the vow most persons make on that blissful occasion called the wedding.

Have you ever wondered where such a vow originated, or if it is still valid and binding today? Can we disregard it with impunity? If it is valid today, to whom does it apply, and are there loopholes?

Is it more scripturally appropriate to use the modern version which says, **"as long as we both shall love"**?

Does the Bible really give us a consistent basis upon which we can stand with confidence and say, *"Thus saith the Lord"*?

Upon reading many of the books on this subject today, one comes away almost convinced that it's open season for opinions (i.e., your guess is as good as mine).

The purpose of my writing this book is based upon the belief that there are many Godly men and women in this generation who are not concerned with what men want to hear—but what the Word of God says. Once these are convinced that there is "an absolute," a bed-rock foundation of scriptural truth, then they will adjust their position accordingly and stand with firm conviction, regardless of the cost.

I do not ask that you judge this book by its literary excellence or scholastic profundity, but rather by its consistency and harmony with all of the Scripture verses pertaining to this subject.

*J*esus Christ has called His Church to set a standard; not to gain a following:

If in setting that standard the Church does gain a following, all the better.

If, however, the Church fails to set the standard and then gains a following, it will be to Her detriment.

Joseph Webb

Jesus said:

Ye are the salt of the earth: but if the salt have lost his savour, wherewith shall it be salted? It is thenceforth good for nothing, but to be cast out, and to be trodden under foot of men.

Matthew 5:13

Introduction

Secular and religious leaders are alarmed at the rapid moral decline being witnessed today in our society. The ripping asunder of marriage relationships has now passed the alarming stage and has reached epidemic proportions. Worse yet is its pandemic rise in the professing Bible believing churches of our nation. One of the fastest areas of increase in divorces percentage-wise today, is among ministers and their wives.

What we are seeing develop in churches now is only *"a sowing the wind"* (Hosea 8:7) and unless the Church of Jesus Christ returns to a historically consistent Biblical position concerning marriage and divorce, we will witness the *"reaping of a whirlwind"* beyond our wildest imagination. Part of that whirlwind is already becoming evident. The majority of juvenile crimes and drug-related arrests in our country today are committed by those reared in broken homes.

Recent psychological studies also show that three out of four children coming from broken homes will repeat the pattern of their parents when they establish their own homes. Thus, the truth of Exodus 34 becomes evident.

Exodus 34:7b
*"...visiting the iniquity of the fathers **upon the children,** and upon the children's children, unto the third and to the fourth generation."*

If this nation's churches won't stem the tide of this plague with the uncompromising truth of God's Word, then the warning that Jesus gave may become a reality in the next generation.

Luke 14:34-35

"Salt is good: but if the salt have lost his savour, wherewith shall it be seasoned? It is neither fit for the land, nor yet for the dunghill; but men cast it out. He that hath ears to hear, let him hear."

There **is** a clear answer in the Word of God. **It will not be an easy answer,** but a sure one. Many will have to **unlearn** much of what they have accepted in the past as **gospel.** They will have to quit looking at the **experiences of men**, and get back to *"thus saith the Lord."* Some who receive this truth will pay a dear price in present ministries if they preach it, but it will be worth the price when harvest time comes.

In studying church history we find that every time God **restored truth to the church**, those who were willing to adjust their theology to agree with God's Word paid a great price. Yet, God has always honored those servants who were willing to stand on His Word, regardless of the cost. The late A. W. Tozer stated it well when he said,

"Bible exposition without moral application raises no opposition. It is only when the hearer is made to understand that truth is in conflict with his heart, that resistance sets in. As long as people can hear orthodoxy divorced from life, they will attend and support churches and institutions without objection. On the other hand, the man who preaches truth and applies it to the lives of his hearers, will feel the nails and the thorns. He will lead a hard life, but a glorious one."[1]

Anyone who has dared to stand against the tide of popular theology knows whereof we speak. After years of research and Bible study concerning marriage and divorce, I am of the

---

[1] Quotes by A. W. Tozer from material copyrighted by Christian Publications, Inc. Used by permission.

conviction that this teaching is scripturally sound and socially electrifying. There has been a price to pay, and nails and thorns to feel. Because I have preached it, I have seen the fruit of this message in the lives of those with seeming **irreconcilable circumstances** being **reconciled**. I have seen young people, who hearing it for the first time, are suddenly realizing the awesome seriousness of stepping into a lifetime commitment—**marriage**. The price tag of obedience has been worth it a thousand times over because, *"Obedience is better than sacrifice."*

Please read this book with your Bible open, and ask the Holy Spirit to witness it's truth to your heart. To accept my opinions on this subject will not suffice. Only accept what the Word of God consistently declares from Genesis through Revelation.

John 8:32
"And ye shall know the Truth and the Truth shall make you free."

John 17:17
"Thy Word is Truth."

Table of Contents

And the Lord God said, it is not good that man should be alone; I will make him an help meet for him. And Adam said, This is now bone of my bones, and flesh of my flesh: she shall be called Woman, because she was taken out of Man. Therefore shall a man leave his father and his mother, and shall cleave unto his wife: And they shall be one flesh.

Genesis 2:18, 23, 24

Section I

How Marriage Began

Except the Lord build the house they labour in vain that build it: except the Lord keep the city, the watchman waketh but in vain.

Psalms 127:1

Chapter 1

The Origin of Marriage

Before we can determine an answer to today's problem of divorce and multiple marriages in our society, we must go to the root, the foundation, **the beginning of the practice of marriage**. We must know:

- ☞ **Its origin**
- ☞ **Its originator**

If we miss here, we are building beautiful air castles of men's ideas with no permanent foundation or solution. Any solution **must** be based solely upon the complete revelation in God's Word.

I. God's word teaches that marriage is a divine institution.

A. Its Origin:

In Genesis 2, we find **the only reliable resource material** to establish **the basis** for **the origin** of the institution of marriage. Other books will expound theories and philosophies concerning human relationships, but only God's Word gives historical fact. In verse 18, God made a decision.

Genesis 2:18

"And the Lord God said, It is not good that the man should be alone; I will make him an help meet for him."

So the Lord put Adam to sleep and took one of his ribs and made a woman.

Genesis 2:22

"...and brought her unto the man."

This reveals the historic conception of marriage.

B. Its Originator:

It's important to note that the Bible says God created man and woman as sexual beings. Contrary to what some might think, God was not asleep or on vacation when sex was invented. He created sex as a pure, beautiful experience. Thus, when God presented Eve to Adam, He became the world's first matchmaker. Marriage was **originated**, or divinely **founded by God**, for **all** men and women. He conceived marriage as a covenant without any input from the creature (man). Although **people marry people**, only God can make two one flesh based upon the terms of the covenant found in Genesis 2:22-24.

II. God's word teaches that marriage is a declared institution.

The Bible shows that up to this time there was a woman and a man, two **separate** individuals—not *"one flesh."* Refer to Illustration #1.

Illustration #1

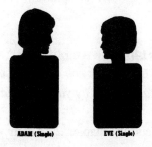

ADAM (Single)   EVE (Single)

Then Adam made a confession of acceptance.

Genesis 2:23
"And Adam said, This is now (When? **Now!**)
*bone of my bones, and flesh of my flesh: she shall
be called Woman."*

When this **declaration of acceptance** was made, **a
divine miracle took place.** Two individuals were made
"one flesh" by God. **Refer to Illustration #2.** This is
confirmed by Malachi when he stated that God was
displeased with the Jewish people because they had *"dealt
treacherously"* with their wives.

Illustration #2

ADAM (Married) EVE

Malachi 2:14b

*"Yet is she thy companion, and the wife **of thy covenant.**"*

Malachi 2:14b (The Amplified Bible)

"Yet she is your companion and the wife of your covenant [made by your marriage vows]."

Back in Genesis Chapter 2, Adam **verbally received** Eve as his helpmeet, and **God made them** *"one flesh."* **Don't miss this truth**; don't take it lightly. This **vow** or act of acceptance by Adam is vital if we are to understand God's basis and process of uniting two persons in marriage. Genesis 2:24 says, *"Therefore..."* (When it says *"therefore,"* find out what it is there for.) A transaction just took place here between Adam, Eve, and God. The **end result** of that verbal transaction is explained.

Genesis 2:24

"Therefore shall a man leave his father and his mother, and shall cleave unto his wife: and they shall be one flesh."

God divinely **originated** and **established** the **institution of marriage**, and made Adam and Eve *"one flesh"* by **a declared intention** or vow, by Adam. There was no government official, no pastor, priest, or rabbi. It was **a sovereign act of God**.

Today a minister, a Justice of the Peace, or Notary Public will say, "Forasmuch as you, Jack, and you, Jill, have consented (mutually agreed) together, and have committed your faith to each other (covenanted or vowed) **in the presence of God** and these witnesses, and have confirmed the same by giving and receiving rings, and joining hands...I therefore **pronounce you** (not **join you**, but **pronounce you**) husband and wife."

Upon what authority is another person able to say this? Only upon the authority that **the vows were made**. This authority is based upon God's Word in Genesis 2. When Jack and Jill make these vows, God unites the two to become one. In Mark 10: 6-9, Jesus confirmed this original experience as God's perfect plan,

Mark 10:6-9
*"But from the beginning of the creation **God made them** male and female. For this cause shall a man leave his father and mother, and cleave to his wife, and they twain shall be **one flesh:** so then they are **no more twain, but one flesh**. What therefore **God hath joined together**, let not man put asunder."*

Note several things.
First, the verbal confession which was spoken by Adam in the garden and reaffirmed by Jesus Christ resulted in a *"one flesh"* situation.

Second, the act of making them *"one flesh"* was an act of God, not man.

Mark 10:7
*"For this cause shall a man **leave** his father and mother, and **cleave** to his wife."*

The word *"cleave"* in the Greek is **proskollaomai** and means to be cemented, glued, or joined fast to, thus implying a **relationship of permanency**.

Mark 10:9

*"What therefore **God** hath **joined** (literally: yoked together..."*

Third, it was **a permanent gluing** (joining or yoking).

Mark 10:9b

"...let not man put asunder."

It's interesting how the Living Bible brings out the force of the Greek even more strongly.

Mark 10:9b (Living Bible)

"...no man may separate what God has joined together."

As we continue to study all the pertinent verses concerning marriage, we will see that God's Word consistently agrees with what I am saying. God, who **originated marriage** and established the rules by which it was to operate, **created the first union** with Adam and Eve. Only God can create a *"one flesh"* relationship between two persons. Know further that, that *"one flesh"* condition is created **through the making of a vow.**

*S*on of man, I have made thee a watch-man...therefore hear the word at my mouth, and give them warning from me.

Ezekiel 3:17

*T*he work of God's watchman is not to delight, pacify, or titillate those under his care. His task instead is to let his voice, like a trumpet, reverberate a clear, articulate alarm whenever the enemy appears. That trumpet call must not infer uncertainty or doubt, but rouse the city to definite action. If the watchman fails here, the blood of the city will be on his hands, and the shame of his failure will never leave him.

O watchman, sound the warning, the enemy is already in the city.

Joseph Webb

Chapter 2

The Universality of the Marriage Law

Chapter One's study of Scripture shows that *"in the beginning"*

☞ God originated marriage as a divine institution.
☞ God established the rules for uniting a man and a woman into one flesh through their vows.
☞ God clearly declared that the duration of the uniting is for life.

I. Area of Application:

The next vital question for which we must find a scriptural answer is—To **whom** does this marriage law **apply**?

Amazingly, there are some today who teach that Biblical marriage laws apply **only** to Christians, and **then, only** under certain circumstances. According to them, **God doesn't even recognize an unbeliever's marriage**, their divorce, or the families that result from those relationships. They teach that once an unsaved person believes, all former things are as though they were not. Imagine telling that to many unsaved, married friends you know, who have persisted in making their marriages work, when those around them, who profess Christianity, have thrown in the towel and divorced. Imagine telling them it's all useless—meaningless—that God doesn't hold them responsible for the vows they made when they got married. Some people are anxiously looking for such an out today! But God's Word **doesn't say that**!

I'll agree that such a **philosophy of absolution** would be nice, if only it also applied to other areas of men's lives.

If I could go to a man on the street and say:
> "**Only believe,** and your debts, driving you to bankruptcy will be as though they never were. God will supernaturally erase them from all company records."

Or, go to the man on death row, and say:
> "**Only believe,** and the charges against you will be supernaturally erased from all of society's records. You will be free to go home tomorrow, and no one will ever remember your ever having committed the first crime."

If I could say to the young girl, who suddenly finds herself pregnant out of wedlock:
> "**Only believe**, and that unborn baby will disappear, and you'll physically be as though you never sinned. All physical evidences of being pregnant will disappear and your family and friends will miraculously forget it ever happened."

We know that each of these incidents is unrealistic. The arguments that say the unbelievers of this world are in an amoral never-never land, and their conduct is outside of the knowledge of God, are also unrealistic. If that **were** so, upon what basis will there be a Great White Throne Judgment? What will be the *"works"* that are described as being in *"the books,"* that shall be opened in Revelation, Chapter 20? Don't be deceived in this area! There is **not a shred of scriptural evidence** to substantiate it! To **truly** understand the Biblical position of marriage **we must not miss this truth!**

The marriage law was established in the **Garden of Eden.** This was **before** the fall, before Abraham, **before** the Law, and **before** Pentecost. **This marriage law is universal** and applies to **all physical descendants of Adam and Eve.** If you are a descendant of someone else, you are exempt. God established **the marriage law for universal application,** and has never rescinded that law.

I know mankind departed from God's standard in the Old Testament, and we'll deal with that later in the book. But for now, know that **the marriage law** applies to, and is binding upon, believers, unbelievers, men, women, religious, nonreligious, and even sacrilegious—**all** physical descendants of Adam and Eve.

II. Scriptural Illustrations:

A. Look at **Cain**, the son of Adam and Eve. His sacrifice was not pleasing to the Lord, but his brother's was. In the heat of anger and jealously he slew his brother. His descendants, who were classified as wicked, were destroyed in the Noahic flood.

Genesis 4:16-17
"And Cain went out from the presence of the Lord, (does that sound like a believer to you?) *and dwelt in the land of Nod, on the east of Eden. And Cain knew his wife, and she conceived, and bare Enoch..."*

God recognized this marriage when the Bible called her Cain's *"wife."*

13

B. Verse 19 of that same chapter speaks of **Lamech**, the great-great-great-grandson of Cain, committing polygamy:

Genesis 4:19
"And Lamech took unto him two wives…"

C. Again in Genesis Chapter 20, is the story of Abraham and Sarah visiting the land of Gerar. **Abimelech**, the Philistine, King of Gerar, and a descendant of Ham (the son of Noah who was cursed after the flood for shaming his father), took Sarah into his own harem. He felt it was proper, since Abraham told him that Sarah was his sister.

God intervened. In verse 3, He warned the unbelieving pagan Philistine, Abimelech, not to touch Sarah, or he'd be *"a dead man."* God told Abimelech the truth concerning Abraham and Sarah, and Abimelech obeyed quickly. Abimelech gave Abraham a tongue lashing, returned his wife, Sarah, and gave him many gifts. Abraham then prayed for Abimelech, and Genesis Chapter 20, tells us, that God is **very much aware** of unbelievers' marriages.

Genesis 20:17-18
*"…God healed Abimelech, and his **wife**, and his maidservants; **and they bare children**. For the Lord had fast closed up all the wombs of the house of Abimelech…"*

God **does** recognize unbelievers' marriages and their offspring. He **closed the wombs** in warning, and **opened the wombs** in obedience. **The marriage law is universal**, and does **not** apply **only to believers**.

D. Look again in Genesis Chapter 39, at the story of Joseph in Egypt, and Potiphar's wife. Potiphar was an

Egyptian, the captain of Pharaoh's personal guard unit. Potiphar bought **Joseph** as a slave. When he saw how everything Joseph did prospered, he appointed him as overseer of all he owned. Joseph had the run of Potiphar's whole house. He managed every detail of Potiphar's business and domestic interests. All Potiphar paid attention to from day to day was what he ate. Here was a believer, in an unbeliever's home. Potiphar, an Egyptian, certainly cannot be considered a Jew, or a believer in Jehovah. He was merely a shrewd business man, who knew a good thing when he saw it in Joseph.

In Genesis Chapter 39, you can read that **Joseph believed that God recognized an unbeliever's marriage**. Verse 7 says that Potiphar's **wife** propositioned Joseph in her own house, but Joseph, sternly refused. Then in verse 9 he gave two reasons for refusing. First:

> **Genesis 39:9b**
> *"...thou art his wife..."*

Secondly:

> **Genesis 39:9c**
> *"...how then can I do this great wickedness, and sin against God?"*

What Joseph was actually stating in those two given reasons was: (Paraphrased.) "I know the laws of God. I know His marriage law applies universally to **all descendants** of Adam and Eve. Even though I'm not married, I know you and Potiphar pledged yourselves together at some time. I also know that when you pledged yourselves **that my God supernaturally made you and Potiphar** *"one flesh."* Oh, you might not have felt it when it happened, but upon the authority of my God, it did

15

happen. Now, my God says that to violate your union with Potiphar is to violate His **universal marriage law**. I just cannot do that, no matter what the cost."

Then Joseph fled, and when Potiphar came home, his wife accused Joseph of being the agressor. The cost was prison, when Potiphar's wife couldn't stand to be snubbed. Thank God Joseph understood **God's marriage law**, and although **he suffered for obedience** temporarily, God lifted him up and honored him. Wouldn't it be wonderful if there were more men today, especially those involved in the gospel ministry, who were as convinced of this law as was Joseph. I wish all the families of our churches were as convinced of this truth as was Joseph, and feared God in this area as he did. If they were, many of their entertainment appetites and their circle of friends would probably be changed drastically. **May God help more of our ministers today, see this truth.**

E. You can read the story for yourself concerning wicked **King Ahab,** and the help meet he acquired, in I Kings 16. Here was a godless man who:

I Kings 16:30
"did evil in the sight of the Lord above all that were before him."

Yet verse 31 says that God recognized his marriage.

I Kings 16:31, 33
"And it came to pass...he took to wife Jezebel...and went and served Baal, and worshipped him...And Ahab did more to provoke the Lord God of Israel to anger than all the kings of Israel that were before him."

We know that God **unites** all marriages—believers and unbelievers. I didn't say he **approves** of all marriages; I said God **unites** all couples, that vow, or pledge themselves to each other.

Let me insert one more thing here before we go on. The Bible says that God makes them *"one flesh"* when He hears those vows uttered. **From his standpoint**, as He looks down upon that couple, He sees them, **from then on,** as one—*"never again twain"*—or **separate**. This, like the experience of regeneration, happens in the spirit world, and can only be understood with spiritual discernment.

God says in His Word that if I repent of my sins, believe Jesus Christ died for my sins, and invite Christ into my life as Lord and Master, I'll be saved. He says that when that happens I will suddenly be *"in Christ,"* and Christ will be *"in me."* He goes on to say that *"I am seated in heavenly places in Christ Jesus."* When the Father sees me, He sees me *"clothed in the righteousness of Christ." Even though we can't explain these things in the natural, still they are very real, and we must accept them by faith, because the word of God says so.*

In the same way, although I can't explain it, God's Word teaches that every person, who, each for the first time, covenants with another in a heterosexual relationship, and who is a descendant of Adam and Eve, comes under **the marriage law.** They **become** *"one flesh"* in His sight. **Please don't miss this important truth!**

Let me give you more examples lest you think I have exhausted this truth from the Scriptures already.

F. In **Daniel Chapter 6**, the Word tells of Daniel being thrown into the lions' den. The magicians tricked the King of the Medes and Persians to enact an edict, making it illegal to bow down to anyone but the King. Anyone violating this edict was to be thrown into the lions' den. The magicians knew Daniel was a godly man and was blameless in every other way. They devised their plan, to get rid of this godly man, whom they despised.

After Daniel spent a night in a den full of lions, whose mouths God had closed, the King gladly brought Daniel up out of the den the next morning, and acknowledged that Daniel's God had preserved him. The King also saw through the other men's plot, and its purpose.

Daniel 6:24

*"And the King commanded, and they brought **those men** which had accused Daniel, and they cast them into the den of lions,* (**watch now**!) ***them, their children, and their wives...***"

If God doesn't recognize unbelievers' marriages, why didn't it say *"their women,"* **instead of** *"their wives?"*

Let's go over into **the New Testament** and see if this truth carries over.

G. In Matthew 14:1-4, we have the story of **John the Baptist** confronting Herod and Herodias. Herod, who was half Indumean and half Samaritan, was a drunken, immoral, paganistic despot. He had seen fit to steal away his brother Phillip's wife, Herodias.

John the Baptist stood up to Herod and Herodias over this matter, and was beheaded for his conviction.

Who said, **"What you don't know, won't hurt you?"** In verse 4, John said to Herod:

Matthew 14:4

*"...It is **not lawful** for thee to have her."*

What law was John speaking of here? Certainly not the Law of the half Indumean and half Samaritan. Certainly not

18

the Law of the Romans, nor just the Jewish commandments. John knew **the universal marriage law** applied to *"all flesh"*, and by the anger it stirred in Herodias, she evidently knew of the Law too. John didn't need to set up a one or two week seminar to teach these pagans this truth. They knew what he said was so, and didn't like it.

Some seminars are taking days and weeks to try to persuade people today that this Law doesn't exist. **Don't you believe it!** The seminars will cease, but God's Word is settled forever in the heavens.

H. In Matthew Chapter 27, God recognized another unbeliever's marriage. When **Pilate** sat on the judgment seat, trying Jesus Christ, had he been a wise man, he could have saved himself a lot of trouble. But being like many married men I know, he turned a deaf ear to his best friend, his wife.

Matthew 27:19

*"...**his wife** sent unto him, saying, Have thou nothing to do with that just man..."*

Who would say that Pilate and his wife were believers? None should. Yet, God recognized their *"one flesh"* condition. When God looked down upon them, He saw Pilate *"one flesh"* with his **"wife."**

It amazes me how men can say that God doesn't recognize, or see the marriages and divorces of the unsaved. Yet, these same people will preach that God **puts up** rulers, and **puts down** rulers. They say that both evil and godly rulers are there by divine appointment, and that God rules in the affairs of the nations. They preach that we are to obey the laws of the land. This is speaking of secular laws, rules, and rulers. They preach we are to obey them, and pray for them that, we might live peaceable lives. May God help us to see that **God is sovereign over**, and **aware of**, all His creation. Scripture teaches us that man's every word, thought, and deed is recorded by God. The Scripture goes on to declare:

Matthew 12:36
"But I say unto you, That every idle word that men shall speak, they shall give account thereof in the day of judgment"

I. One more example is found in Luke Chapter 17. It tells of the *"days of Noah,"* and describes the unbelievers who perished in the flood:

Luke 17:27
*"They did eat, they drank, they **married wives,** they were **given in marriage**, until the day that Noah entered into the ark, and the flood came and destroyed them all."*

All those destroyed by the flood, were just like unbelievers today, typical people who reject God's message of repentance and forgiveness. When they married, **God knew they married**; *"They married wives..."* When they divorced, God knew they divorced:

Genesis 6:5,9
"And God saw the wickedness of men was great in the earth, and that every imagination of the thoughts of his heart was only evil continually."

In verse 9, it implies that the bloodlines of all the people from Adam and Eve up to Noah's time, were corrupted. God said in Genesis 6:5, *"The wickedness of man was great in the earth, and that every imagination of the thoughts of his heart was only evil continually.* " Consequently, God said that Noah was **the only one left** who was *"perfect in his generations"*; or upright in his generations. God's answer to his corruption, was found in verse 7, *"I will destroy man, whom I have created...but Noah found grace in the eyes of the Lord."* God knew all other families were corrupted.

If they lied, cheated, stole, raped, killed, **whatever**, it was recorded in *"the books"* Revelation 20:12, and they will be judged *"according to their works."* If they had wives, *"help meets;"* **by what law** did they have wives? Who established that law? If God saw them as husbands and wives in their unsaved state, He saw them as *"one flesh,"* didn't He? If He saw them as *"one flesh"*, **who** made them that way? Certainly **not** the government, **not** a sexual relationship, **not** the person who officiated the ceremony—whatever that might have been in those godless societies; **only God** could have performed this act. **He alone** established **the universal marriage law,** for **He alone** makes two *"one flesh."*

Whoever you are—**wherever** you are—**whenever** you consented or vowed yourself to another person of the opposite sex for the first time, before a government official, or minister of the Gospel, **know** that a **supernatural happening** took place, similar to the miracle of the new birth. Just as God causes a repentant sinner to be *"in Christ;"* even so He makes two persons *"one flesh."* The God of all creation is a God of covenants, and understands the meaning of covenants. It behooves mankind to seek to understand the seriousness of **physical and spiritual covenant relationships,** as they are presented to us in God's Word. The Word is to be *"a lamp unto our feet and a light unto our path."* (Psalm 119:105)

If God **never** recognizes unbelievers' marriages, then **it would be impossible** for **unbelievers** to ever be **adulterers.** A simple definition of an adulterer is: **one who has sex**

relations outside of the marriage relationship, otherwise described **as extra-marital relationships.**

If **unbelievers** can't be adulterers, as some infer, then all Scripture referring to adultery, would have to refer **only to believers.** If that is so, we have a real problem trying to explain the following verses.

> **I Corinthians 6:9-10**
> *"Be not deceived: neither... **Adulterers...** shall inherit the kingdom of God."*

If that only applies to born-again believers, then it's saying that **only redeemed people** will not inherit the Kingdom of God. Doesn't that sound rather ridiculous?

You can easily see that this doctrinal position creates many **irreconcilable distortions of Scripture.**

III. Additional Insights:

Before we go on to the next chapter, let me emphasize another point. I've tried to show you from Scripture, that **God** makes a man and woman, that covenant themselves together, husband and wife, or *"one flesh."* Please note that God does not say, He makes them one **mind,** one **spirit** or one **attitude.** He only says that **after the vow or mutual commitment, He sees** them from then on as *"one flesh."* The other areas of mind, spirit and attitude, He leaves up to you both, to work out during a lifetime of adjusting to each other.

I'm sure those of you who are married, realize that it is fantasy to think that **all strife ceases** once you make your vows, and finally get that ring on your finger. Neither is it realistic to think that tranquility reigns, when the one officiating at the ceremony says, "I now pronounce you husband and wife." To believe that the storms of life will all subside, and peace and perpetual happiness will permeate that quiet little love-nest, like syrup covers pancakes, is fantasy. **I hope you don't believe that...!** God's Word **never** said it would be like that. That's why men and women need the Holy Spirit to keep them through the hard times. He will bring into their lives, **Biblical principles,** by which they may operate and be strengthened together, in the storms of life that **will come.**

When I see unbelievers weather the storms of adjusting to married life, and loving one another dearly, I take my hat off to them. For they *"which have not the law, do by nature those things contained in the law."* (Romans 2:14) Those same unbelievers, put those who **know** the law, and aren't following it, to open shame.

The Body of Christ needs to know that God uses those pressures of adjusting to another's disposition and tastes, to help us mature for His glory. The *"one flesh"* relationship is **the only foundation** upon which God wants a man and woman to build. For God said:

Genesis 2:18
"...It is not good that the man should be alone; I will make him an help meet for him."

Some of you may be saying, "maybe God made us *'one flesh,'* but **there's no foundation left** on which we can build anymore."

May I encourage you to get this truth settled once and for all in your soul. **If you vowed** yourself once to a partner, and that partner had never vowed himself, or herself, to another before you, God **did** make you *"one flesh."* That's true whether you were saved, unsaved, black, white, rich, poor, simple, educated, or whatever. **God made you** *"one flesh."* If you see **that**, you are acknowledging a divine miracle. You're declaring that God can perform supernatural miracles. How else can you explain two as one?

It makes no difference what has happened since that day you were united...the hurts, the hates, the wounds, the distrust. The God who made you *"one flesh"* is **a miracle-working God**. He can **resurrect** dead emotion. He can **calm** the storms, and **heal** irreparable wounds. He will **not** work those miracles for you, until you are **convinced** that:

- ☞ God instituted your marriage
- ☞ He alone makes two *"one flesh"* by their vows
- ☞ By working through your struggle, the two of you will be better people.

For, like Peter of old, **after** you have been *"sifted"* and recover, you can *"strengthen your brethren,"* (Luke 22:32) and experience a restoration of love, trust and forgiveness, never before imagined.

Some may say, "It's too late. **I have no feeling** for him or her anymore. The love is gone, the emotion is dead!" **Contrary to popular belief,** and most present-day teaching, **love** is **not** an **emotion**; although it may **result** in emotional feelings; but **love is a decision**.

We decide, and promise God, to love our marriage partner for life, for better or worse, richer or poorer, in sickness and in health, **regardless of their conduct**. That has to be **a decision**. I call it a **quality decision**. A quality decision, is a decision, when once made, **eliminates** the need to make many other decisions.

When I decided to love my wife, I never had to decide again if I'd ask another girl for a date, or whether I would flirt, etc. My **quality decision** freed me from having to even consider those possibilities again.

Whenever one says, "I **can't** love him (or her) anymore." They are actually saying, "I **won't** love him (or her) anymore." When someone says that, they are making a moral decision, contrary to the known will of God, this is **rebellion,** and shall be judged as such by God.

Chapter 3

Covenants and Vows

Up till now we have said:

☞ **God** originated marriage as a divine institution.
☞ **God** established the uniting of a man and a woman into one flesh by their vows.
☞ **God** clearly declared the duration of that uniting to be for life.
☞ **God** originated the marriage law in the Garden of Eden, and thus it's application is **universal in scope** upon all the offspring of Adam and Eve.

We've shown from Scripture, that a *"one flesh"* relationship is **a supernatural act of God**, whereby, **He** causes two individuals, to become one. This miracle takes place when any two persons (a man and a woman), come together, and each for the first time, consent and promise, covenant, pledge, or vow themselves to each other.

Let me put these truths into one definition of marriage. This definition is a compilation of many others, trying to embrace what has been said thus far.

I. A Definition of Marriage:

"Marriage is a universal process of divine origin and regulation, by which a man and a woman, by mutual

consent, are united by God, for the purpose of living together permanently, in love, in order to establish and maintain a home and a family."

A. "Marriage is a universal process of divine origin and regulation…"

This says that God was the **originator** of **the marriage law**, and His rules, established in the Scriptures, have **universal application** to **all** descendants of Adam and Eve. It implies that **all** descendants of Adam and Eve, are thus **subject** to these rules, and shall be **judged** by them.

B. "By which a man and a woman…"

Since the application of the marriage law is **universal**, we do not say that it just applies to any Christian, Jewish, or other religious man or woman. Being **universal in scope**, it applies to **every man and woman**. Thus, the definition says, "a man and a woman." This **would not** be applicable to a man and a man, or a woman and a woman. Such relationships are **condemned and forbidden** in Scripture. Genesis 13:13, Deuteronomy 23:17,18, Romans 1:26-32.

C. "By mutual consent…"

It is **the agreeing** of the bride and groom, to give each to the other, that constitutes the uniting, or *"one flesh"* union by God.

Malachi 2:14 (The Amplified Bible)
"yet she is your companion, and the wife of your covenant" [made by your marriage vows].

D. "Are united by God"

Only God can make two *"one flesh."* The **only** *"joining,"* or *"one flesh"* relationship described in the Word of God, is **"for life."**

1. Sex Relations Do Not Establish the *"One Flesh"* Relationship.

Sex relations, are only a **privilege** of marriage and **do not establish it**. Matthew makes this clear, when he speaks of Joseph and Mary. When Joseph learned that Mary was with child, he was going to **divorce her.** I will speak more of this divorcing in a later chapter. Then, the angel told him the child was of the Holy Spirit, and that he should marry her.

> **Matthew 1:24**
> *"Then Joseph being raised from sleep did as the angel of the Lord had bidden him, and took unto him his wife:"*

> **Matthew 1:24 (The Living Bible)**
> *"...brought Mary home to be his wife."*

> **Matthew 1:24 (The Amplified Bible)**
> *"...he took [her to his side as] his wife,"*

They were married; they were *"one flesh,"* husband and wife, and yet verse 25 says:

> **Matthew 1:25**
> *"And knew her not..."*

27

This speaks of a physical knowing. They had **no sex relations,** even though they were already *"one flesh."*

Until when?

Matthew 1:25
"...till she had brought forth her firstborn son..."

Matthew 1:25 (The Living Bible)
*"...but she remained a virgin **until her son was born...**"*

Matthew 1:25 (The Amplified Bible)
"But he had no union with her as her husband until she had brought forth her first-born Son..."

Therefore, Scripture teaches that **sex relations** do not **make a marriage.** Joseph and Mary, were legally married for months, before Joseph *"knew her."*

Other Biblical examples proving that sex does not make *"one flesh"* would be:
- ☞ David and Bathsheba: II Samuel 11
- ☞ The woman caught in adultery: John 8
- ☞ Christ's teaching: Luke 16:18

Luke 16:18 (The Living Bible)
*"So anyone who divorces his wife and **marries** someone else."*

The use of the word *"**marries,**"* clearly implies that **sex was involved** in the second relationship. Yet Jesus didn't say they were *"joined,"* or became *"one flesh."* Instead he said they *"committed adultery."* That does not **sound** as though **sex** makes two people *"one flesh."*

Common sense tells us, that if sex relations constitutes marriage, then there would be no such thing as fornication. If the physical act makes a couple *"one flesh,"* then the moment the **physical act** takes place, that act would make that man and woman *"one flesh,"* and it would be honorable. Common sense, however, tells us this isn't so.

I Corinthians 6:16 sounds like sex does make two, one.

I Corinthians 6:16
"...he which is joined to an harlot is one body? for two, saith he, shall be one flesh."

The key word to this verse is *"joined,"* which comes from the Greek word ***kollaomai***. That Greek word, comes from the root word ***kollao***, which means to glue or cement together. Compare this with the Greek word for *"cleave,"* which is ***proskollao***. This also comes from the same root word ***kollao***. Vine, in his Expository Dictionary, says this word is, "a strengthened form of ***kollao***, with ***pros***, to, intensive, is used in the passive voice, reflexively, in a metaphorical sense."[2]

This same strengthened word, ***proskollao***, is used also in Ephesians, concerning the relationship between a husband and wife.

---

[2]Quotes from Vine's Expository Dictionary of Old and New Testament Words: Copyright 1981, Baker Publishing Company, Ada, Michigan. Used by Permission.

Ephesians 5:31

   "Shall be joined unto his wife, and they two shall be one flesh."

This joining speaks of a permanent kind of binding, gluing, or being cemented, as in Matthew 19:5,6 and Mark 10:7, where it speaks clearly of the ***marriage union*** being for life, *"wherefore they are no more twain"* (never again two). It's simply stating that if a man is married, or "glued" to a woman, and then finds out she's a harlot, she's still his wife, and *"one flesh,"* with him. It is God that makes them *"one flesh"* **by their vow**.

   Scriptural proof that sex does not establish a "one flesh" relationship, is found in the following texts.

   In Genesis Chapter 38 is the story of **Judah**. Judah had three sons: Er, Onan, and Shelah. Er was married to Tamar (verse 6), but before they could have children, the Lord slew Er, because of his wickedness (verse 7). Then, as was the custom in that day, Judah told his next oldest son, Onan, to marry Tamar, and produce a child to carry on his brother's name (verse 8). Onan disobeyed his father, due to his own selfishness, and spilled the sperm upon the ground. The Lord slew him (verses 9, 10). Then Judah told Tamar to wait for his youngest son. Tamar soon saw that Shelah was not going to fulfill his duty either. When Tamar heard that Judah's wife had died, she found out where Judah was going. Being desperate to raise up a child in her husband's name, she disguised herself as a harlot and seduced Judah on the road. For her services, she took his ring, bracelets, and staff as collateral, until Judah could send her his payment, and recover his personal items (verses 12-18).

Later, when Judah heard that Tamar was pregnant, he commanded that she be burned with fire (verse 24). At this time, Tamar brought forth the items of collateral, to show Judah that **he** was the father of the twins that were to be born (verse 25).

Then Judah acknowledged that he was in the wrong, and not she. **But note**: Neither Judah nor Tamar intimated that his sex relations with Tamar (who performed the services of a **harlot**), caused them to be *"joined"* as *"one flesh."*

Instead, their relationship was then returned to what it was previously .

Genesis 38:26b
"And he knew her again no more."

The same principle holds true with **Sampson and Delilah**.

Judges 16:1
"Then went Sampson to Gaza, and saw there an harlot, and went in unto her."

Judges 16:1 (The Living Bible)
"...spent the night with a prostitute."

Nowhere is it ever intimated that Sampson **ever** became *"joined,"* or *"one flesh"* with Delilah, through his sexual encounter with her, in her profession as a harlot.

In the book of Hosea, the Lord commanded **Hosea** to marry Gomer. Even though she played the harlot, Hosea was still married to her because of their vows. Hosea continued to love and forgive her.

In I Corinthians Chapter 6, **Paul was not saying that sex relations make** *"one flesh,"* but rather that **the joining** of a man to a woman, by their vows, makes them *"one flesh,"* even if she's a harlot. (I Corinthians 6:16) *"For two, sayeth he, shall be one flesh."* There is no doubt that this refers back to Genesis 2:23,24, when Adam accepted Eve, and God spoke these words. May I suggest, that apparently, no sexual union had yet taken place when these words were spoken, but Adam and Eve were **already one flesh.** In fact, the only scriptural reference we find of Adam and Eve having conjugal relations, is after the fall, in Genesis 4:1. *"And Adam knew Eve his wife; and she conceived, and bore Cain, and said, I have gotten a man from the Lord."*

Somehow, we must **remove** from the church's teaching, the concept that sex creates the one flesh relationship. I Corinthians 6:16, is the only verse, when misinterpreted, that even suggests such a thing. God's word **only** uses that phrase, *"one flesh,"* when it is speaking of marriage; **not an illicit affair.**

In the surrounding context, (I Corinthians 6:13-18) Jesus is referring to *"fornication,"* in its broadest sense. This use would include all moral unchastity, in contrast to the definitive use. (I will elaborate on these uses of the term "fornication" later in this book.) His conclusion, is to separate yourself from all moral uncleaness, but know, that if you marry, even a harlot, you become one flesh with her!

Next, realize:

2. The Church Does Not Create or Establish the "One Flesh" Relationship.

If the church or government made a couple *"one flesh,"* then the early saints were in trouble. History tells us that the New Testament Church took **no responsibility for performing** marriage ceremonies, **within the church,** for at least the first 300 years after Christ. Therefore, no one back then could say that the **preacher** or the state made them *"one flesh."*

In 1300 A.D., the Roman Church changed that by canon law, when it ruled that a marriage **had to be** performed by a priest, or was invalid. This practice of the church conducting marriages, was carried over into Protestantism by Luther and other Reformationists.

May I suggest, that many of the great problems the Church is facing today, are with the courts, which are claiming that our children are "wards of the State." This misunderstanding, can be traced back to the confusion experienced by many, in the Church.

3. The Government Does Not Create or Establish the *"One Flesh"* Relationship.

The government requires that a license be obtained before a marriage be performed. This is not because it has the power to unite or join the two parties by that license—but only to facilitate bookkeeping for the state. By requiring the license, the marriage is properly recorded, and an orderly, **"legal"** society, can be maintained.

The government will license a judge, a Justice of the Peace, a clerk, or a minister, giving them the authority to preside over a ceremony, and to confirm its authenticity. But, let me assure you, none of these can

33

make two persons become *"one flesh."* Whenever any of these perform or officiate at a marriage ceremony, they receive from the couple, a form, which must be filled out, signed by witnesses, and sent in within 48 hours. Again, this is **not** so the state can make the couple *"one flesh,"* nor does this imply that any of these men presiding over the ceremony can make them *"one flesh."* Its only purpose, is to keep the state's records straight, and to maintain social order.

Here is a legal definition of marriage **by the State**.

"Marriage is the process, by which the legal relationship of husband and wife is constituted, by a mutual contract."

In other words, the State says whenever a couple decides they want to get married, they must place on public record, the fact that they have mutually agreed, or vowed themselves to each other.

Many people think that the State **makes, or establishes**, and therefore may **break** the marriage bond. Since many have believed that lie, they have, by recognizing **court-declared divorces**, agreed that the state can join or separate them. When the state is granted that power, then the **fruit**, or offspring, of that joining, also comes under the state's jurisdiction. The next step for the state, is very logical. If it can join and separate couples by its authority, then it also has the authority to make the offspring of that union, "wards of the state." We are now reaping the fruit of that error, through government intrusion, into all aspects of family life.

4. God Makes Two *"One Flesh."*

May God help us to repent and say what God says. Matthew Chapter 19 very clearly says that God makes two, one:

Matthew 19:6
"What therefore God hath joined together..."

A *"one flesh"* relationship, is only achieved, by God, through the mutual consent of the persons being united.

In Malachi 2:13, God was declaring His displeasure toward the Jewish people, and said that He was rejecting their offerings.

Malachi 2:13 (Living Bible)
"Yet you cover the altar with your tears because the Lord doesn't pay attention to your offerings any more, and you receive no blessing from him."

In verse 14, they were asking, "Why God, are you so upset with us?" God answered thus:

Malachi 2:14
"...Because the Lord hath been witness between thee and the wife of thy youth, against whom thou hast dealt treacherously: yet is she thy companion, and the wife of thy covenant."

Verse 15 goes on to say:

Malachi 2:15
*"And did not **he make one**?"*

God calls the vows or commitments made at the wedding a **covenant. The Amplified Bible makes it even clearer in Malachi 2:14.**

Malachi 2:14 (The Amplified Bible)
*"...Because the Lord was witness **to the covenant** [made at your marriage] between you and the wife of your youth, against whom you have dealt treacherously and to whom you were faithless. Yet* (Note this: God is saying, {paraphrase} In spite of what you've done) *she is your companion and **the wife of your covenant [made by your wedding vows]**."*

Only God, the One who created and established the marriage, by a sovereign divine act, can join a man and a woman; thus, making them *"one flesh"* for life. This **joining,** takes place when they agree, covenant, or vow to accept each other:

- ☞ **not** by sexual relations
- ☞ **not** by the church
- ☞ **not** through the government license
- ☞ **not** by the officiating officer at the wedding but by **an act of God**.

The written paper (license), given by society, merely **confirms** that the act is recorded, and thus legal, orderly, and proper, according to set standards. The presiding official, is simply declaring, upon the fact of established practice, that you have followed proper procedure. But **God alone**, sovereignly, permanently, joins or glues each couple together, and declares its term succinctly—**for life**.

Matthew 19:6

*"Wherefore they are **no more twain**, but one flesh."*

Unless we understand **this foundational truth**, we **cannot properly interpret** the doctrine of marriage. We will wrongly believe, that the **marriage certificate** we received, following the marriage ceremony, made us *"one flesh,"* and therefore, a **divorce certificate** will separate us, and we'll be free to "**start all over again**."

This reasoning is **not biblical**; and thus, **it is false**. May God help us to see this truth clearly. Whoever you are, **whenever** you and another person, each come for the first time to pledge yourselves to each other as husband and wife, in a God-ordained heterosexual relationship, the Lord is the *"witness"* to that commitment; and **He makes** you *"one flesh"* **for life**.

There is no other scripturally **valid** means of becoming *"one flesh,"* because it was **originated** by God Himself, and **cannot** be changed.

Until you completely understand this foundational principle, you will be confused by men's reasonings, as they try to explain away the permanency and divine origin of marriage, conjuring up excuses for divorce, and subsequent relationships.

37

Please review the verses again:

Mark 10:9b (Living Bible)
"*No man may separate what **God has joined together**.*"

Matthew 9:6
"*Wherefore, they are no more twain but one flesh. What therefore **God hath joined together**, let not man put asunder.*"

Malachi 2:15
"*And did not **he** make one?*"

E. "**For the purpose of living together permanently in love...**"

Many times, people say to me, "I didn't understand what I was saying in the ceremony!"

If the verbiage in your ceremony was really that difficult to understand, then **forget for a moment the vows you made,** and answer these questions. When you agreed to marry your partner:

☞ **How many years** did you have in mind living with him/her?

☞ **How long** did you understand marriages **were** to last?

☞ **Did you expect** to go to the marriage license bureau each year to see if your marriage license has expired yet?

☞ **Did you inform your partner** it was to be **a temporary thing** beforehand?

☞ When asked, "wilt thou keep yourself to him/her, **so long as you both shall live**?," did you say

38

"Yes," or "I do"? If so, you are responsible before God. Jesus said in Matthew Chapter 5:

Matthew 5:37 (Amplified Bible)
*"Let your yes be simply yes, and your **no** be simply **no;** anything more than that comes from the evil one."*

People, by nature today, are **covenant-breakers** or *"truce-breakers."* If, however, you question them carefully, **they know** the marriage bond **is** to be **permanent**.

The part of the definition which says **"in love,"** is **not** based on emotion, but an act of the will. **One chooses or decides,** whom he or she will, or will not love, and then builds a mental case, to justify that decision.

This is why God's Word tells Christians to **love on three levels**:

☞ to love their **husbands/wives**,
☞ to love their **neighbors**, and
☞ to love their **enemies**.

Not because **they deserve it**—but because **He requires it**. Because **God is love**, we know it is consistent with God's nature, to love us. He **chose** to love us, just as husbands and wives are expected to **choose** to love each other, **regardless of his/her conduct**.

F. **"In order to establish and maintain a home and family."**

It's God's will for a couple to establish their own nest.

Genesis 2:24

> *"Therefore shall a man **leave** his father and his mother, and shall cleave unto his wife..."*

It's never normal, for two families to live under one roof, for any extended period of time. It's a necessity sometimes, but far from ideal. Establishing a home, requires **mutual respect,** and the recognizing of **proper roles of authority**. Maintaining a home, requires maturity, responsibility, and **a willingness to change**.

I believe you will find this definition of marriage totally consistent with God's Word.

II. The Biblical Doctrine of Covenants and Vows:

The next vital link in understanding the biblical concept of marriage, is what the Bible has to say about **covenants and vows**.

A. Covenants

The God of Abraham is a covenant-making God. He made a **universal covenant,** when He placed the rainbow in the sky, declaring that the earth would never again be destroyed by water. Because God said it, and promised it by a covenant sign, we know the earth will never again be totally destroyed by water. Various other covenants between men were historically common.

1. Salt Covenant

One was a **"salt covenant."** The salt covenant was used, when two persons came to a mutual agreement, and wanted to make it binding. To bind that agreement, each would take a pinch of salt from his salt pouch, and put it in the other person's salt pouch. The only way that covenant could be broken, by either party, was if one of them could prove that he had separated the one person's salt in his pouch, from his own salt. This was a binding covenant.

2. Blood Covenant

Another type of covenant, was made by God, to Abraham. It was called a "**blood covenant**." The only way a blood covenant could be broken, was by the death of one of the two persons making the covenant. Because of this, God didn't have Abraham as a party to the covenant, but made a covenant with Himself, concerning His promises to Abraham. Therefore, because it was a "blood covenant," it cannot be broken, until **God dies**. I know, that a few years ago, it was suggested that God did die, but don't you believe it! I commune with Him regularly, and He's alive! Thus, the Abrahamic covenant is still in force.

Men also made blood covenants with one another. They would make a vow, then cut themselves enough to bring forth blood. Placing the small wounds together, they would intermingle their blood, and those vows became a blood covenant agreement, that could be broken only by the **death of one of the covenantors.**

Another unique feature of the blood covenant, was that each party involved in it, was declaring to the other: "All I have is yours, and all you have is mine." **Note**: This is why God tested Abraham, to see if he was willing to fulfill that covenant with his son, Isaac. (Genesis 22:1-18)

B. Marriage Is A Covenant.

The **marriage covenant,** like the **salt and blood covenants**, is **to remain in force until one of the partners dies**. The **marriage covenant,** is **similar** to the **blood covenant,** inasmuch as the participants imply that, "All I have is yours, and all you have is mine." Both covenants can be broken, but only by the **death** of the other participant. It is like the salt covenant, in that the participants could never separate one person's salt from the other's; thus, **it was permanent**. Even though there are **many similarities** between the other covenants and the marriage covenant, **the marriage covenant is not a blood covenant**, because:

1. Widows can marry again even though they are no longer virgins, and the Lord recognizes their marriage.

2. Couples marry where one or both, because of physical problems, are totally **impotent**, yet they are married.

3. Joseph **married** Mary, Matthew 1:24-26, but **had no sexual relations with her until Jesus was born**. Yet, they were recognized, even by God, as being married, *"one flesh,"* and covenanted together for life.

4. In Jewish society—**the tearing of the hymen,** which took place in *"the bridegroom's chamber,"* immediately following the marriage ceremony and vows, only proved one very important thing to the Jewish man, that his new bride was **truly** a virgin.

It is not the tearing of the hymen, or the resulting blood, but it is **the vows, or mutual commitment made,** that establishes the marriage covenant. **Thus, the marriage covenant is not a blood covenant**, but is a covenant that remains in force, until one of the participants dies. People today do not want to hear this.

Paul the Apostle told us, in II Timothy 3:3, that *"In the last days, men would be **truce breakers**. "* That means they will make a commitment, and casually turn away from it.

In **Romans Chapter 1**, Paul, describes **the nature** of those, who *"professing themselves to be wise, "* and who turn themselves away from God. Again and again the phrase is used:

Romans 1:26
"God gave them up... "

Romans 1:28
"God gave them over to a reprobate mind, to do those things which are not convenient; "

In describing the end results of these persons' decisions, Paul defines some of the **outward evidences**.

Romans 1:31-32
*"Without understanding, **covenant breakers**... Who, knowing the judgment of God, that they which commit such things are worthy of death, not only do the same, but have pleasure in them that do them. "*

In contrast to this nature, we find Jesus advocating to his disciples, absolute honesty and integrity. This took place, **immediately following** one of his teachings on marriage. Look again at Matthew Chapter 5.

Matthew 5:34-37
"But I say unto you, Swear not at all, (Living Bible says, *'Don't make any vows')* neither by heaven; for it is God's throne: Nor by the earth; for it is His*

*footstool: neither by Jerusalem; for it is the city of the great King. Neither shalt thou swear by thy head, because thou canst not make one hair white or black. But let your communication be, Yea, yea; Nay, nay: **for whatsoever is more than these cometh of evil.**"*

Why do you suppose Jesus warns his disciples of **the seriousness of promises or vows** to God?

God's Word has much to say about the **seriousness** of the words we **speak**.

Proverbs 18:21
> *"Death and life are in the power of the tongue..."*

Too many people today, take too lightly the making of a promise. As a result, this nation is paying a dear price.

I can still remember when I was a boy, one seldom had to contract with someone in writing. If a friend said he'd do some job for you, for so much, you didn't need a contract. You just shook hands and it was done. That was **integrity**, **fidelity**, **honesty**...almost lost words today. Just go to a car dealership today, and try buying a car on a handshake. Try to get a man to build you a house, for so much money on a handshake. It rarely happens today. Why? Men are *"covenant-breakers."* Not only is this true in **man-to-man** relationships, but **man-to-God** relationships also.

We need to know what **God expects,** when we covenant or vow **anything**. Then we'll know what Solomon meant when he said:

Proverbs 18:21
> *"Death and life are in the power of the tongue..."*

The World Book Dictionary defines a **vow** as:
☞ **a solemn promise** made to God.

☞ **an act** by which one consecrates, or devotes himself to some act, service, or condition (state of being).

☞ **a promise of fidelity** or constancy (**as in a marriage vow**).

The Bible speaks of **vows** in Numbers Chapter 30.

Numbers 30:2

"*If a man vow a vow unto the Lord, or swear an oath to bind his soul with a bond;* (meaning: if a man **promises** God he will do or will not do something), **He shall not break his word, he shall do according to all that proceedeth out of his mouth.** "

The book of Numbers, Chapter 30, speaks of a young single woman, making a vow in the presence of her father.

Numbers 30:3-4

"*If a woman also vow a vow unto the Lord, and bind herself by a bond, being in her father's house in her youth; and her father **hear** her vow, and her bond wherewith she hath bound her soul, and her father shall hold his peace at her: **then all her vows shall stand, and every bond wherewith she hath bound her soul shall stand.** "*

Again in Deuteronomy Chapter 23 it states:

Deuteronomy 23:21-23

"*When thou shalt vow a vow unto the Lord thy God, thou shalt not slack to pay it: **for the Lord thy God will surely require it of thee;** and it would be sin in thee. But if thou shalt forbear to vow, it shall be no* *sin in thee. That which is gone out of thy lips thou shalt keep and perform; even a freewill offering, according as thou hast vowed unto the Lord thy God, which thou hast promised with thy mouth."*

Many are not even aware that promises made in a marriage ceremony, are acted upon by God, who created marriage.

When one agrees to marriage, they buy a franchise in **a closed corporation**. God created it, established the rules, is still Chairman of the Board, and has not abdicated any power of attorney. He designed and created mankind. He knew that we were social creatures, that needed an intimate relationship, with another person. Thus, God established the marriage bond. When anyone **agrees to it**, God makes them *"one flesh."* If He didn't make them *"one flesh,"* then their relationship would be one of **fornication**, for **only God** performs this miracle. If any person makes a promise to enter into marriage, He takes them at their word. If a young lady makes a promise to enter into marriage, and her father doesn't stop it, God will take her at her word (Numbers 30:2-5).

After learning these truths, some may plead ignorance and say, **"it was a terrible mistake."** If so, they must consider another warning from God's word.

Ecclesiastes 5:4-7

*"When thou vowest a vow unto God, defer not to pay it; for He hath no pleasure in fools: Pay that which thou hast vowed. Better is it that thou shouldest not vow, than that thou shouldest vow and not pay. Suffer not thy mouth to cause thy flesh to sin; **neither say thou** before the angel, that **it was an error:** wherefore should God be angry at thy voice, **and destroy the work of thine hands?**...but **fear thou God."***

A scriptural example, of the seriousness with which vows were made, is found in the book of Judges. In Chapter 11, is the story of Jephthah, the Gileadite, the son of a harlot. Because of his mother's reputation, Jephthah and his family were outcasts from Israel's society. When the Ammonites threatened Israel, the Israelites knew that Jephthah was a man of valor. Swallowing their pride, they went to Jephthah and asked if he would lead them into battle. After much heart searching, Jephthah agreed, and started out to battle. On the way to battle he spoke an unnecessary vow before he thought it through.

Judges 11:30-32

"And Jephthah vowed a vow unto the Lord, and said, If thou shalt without fail deliver the children of Ammon into mine hands, Then it shall be, that whatsoever cometh forth of the doors of my house to meet me, when I return in peace from the children of Ammon, **shall surely be the Lord's,** *and* **I will offer it up for a burnt offering**...*The Lord delivered them* (the Ammonites) *into his hands."*

He won the victory! Someone said it this way: "Jephthah danced and now he had to pay the fiddler." Jephthah didn't **have to** make the vow he made, **but he did**.

I've tried to put myself in his shoes, by imagining what he might have been thinking, on his way home from battle. I know what some **would** have been thinking on the way home, by what they do when they make other promises. "Well Lord, I know what I said about tithing, but I didn't know the interest would go up on my boat loan." **Or**, "I know I said that I'd preach for you Lord, but I didn't realize **then,** that this scholarship, or this job opportunity, would come along. You understand, Lord."

And **then** there is, "I know I told you in the jungles of Vietnam, or the deserts of Saudi Arabia, that if you'd get me out alive, I'd serve you the rest of my life. However, you understand that I was scared then, and besides, I've got a lot of catching up to do."

Let me say that **right here** is the place, where I believe many a saint has met his Waterloo. Many people have, **somewhere** in the past, made a vow to God and **forgotten it**. May I say in love, **God hasn't forgotten it**. Those same people will never know the full joy of an obedient walk, until they go back and deal with that vow, as Jephthah had to do.

I still remember a young lady, who attended the same college I attended, years ago. She came to the school with a child, and rented her own apartment. During a week of revival services, this girl stood sobbing before the student body, and said:

> "I want you all to know that years ago, I committed my life to serve Christ on the mission field. I ate and slept that dream, until my senior year in high school. Then I met this young man. He wasn't a Christian, but I believed all of Satan's lies, and continued on into that relationship. I was warned over and over again. My devotional life slipped away. My prayer life was an array of desperate cries for God to have patience with me, while I did my own thing. I sowed to the flesh and reaped corruption. The rest is evident," she said as she motioned toward the small child next to her. "I only hope that somehow, God can still use me on the mission field. Oh, **please don't break your promises to God!**"

I'll never forget the hush that came over that audience that day. Here was one who had made a vow to God, had broken it, had repented, and was trying to pick up the pieces.

I can't help but think, that Jephthah, wished he hadn't said what he had, **but he did**. Don't you imagine his thoughts went something like this, on the way home? "Well, maybe my wife will be sweeping when I get home, and will sweep a chicken out the door." Or, "I'll bet old Rover, my hunting dog, will hear me coming; and he'll burst out through the door, to greet me. Then, I can offer the chicken or Rover to the Lord, as a burnt offering, and be free from this vow that I made."

The Word of God says that it didn't happen like that. Instead, this is what did happen, in Jephthah's situation.

Judges 11:34
*"And Jephthah came to Mizpah unto his house, and, behold, **his daughter** came out to meet him with timbrels and with dances: and **she was his only child**."*

Jephthah knew what he had done.

Judges 11:35
*"I have opened my mouth unto the Lord, and **I cannot go back**."*

Judges 11:39 says:
"...she returned unto her father, (Jephthah) who did with her according to his vow which he vowed..."

What did he vow?

Judges 11:31b
*"...I will offer it up for **a burnt offering**."*

49

I'm not here to justify or condemn Jephthah. God will do that. I'm just trying to show you, that **a vow to God,** is a **very serious thing**. Remember:

Ecclesiastes 5:5
> *"Better is it that **thou shouldest not vow,** than that thou shouldest vow **and not pay**."*

I know of no other place in Scripture, where there **may have been** a human burnt sacrifice, but there may have been one here, because a man understood **the seriousness of a vow**.

Judges 11:35b
> *"I have opened my mouth unto the Lord, and I cannot go back."*

I know some say it couldn't possibly mean that Jephthah was required to make an actual human burnt offering. They think it means that his daughter would be dedicated for life to temple service. Since it was his only daughter, the punishment would be that she could never marry. Thus, he would have no grandchildren.

The true substance or meaning of his words are not the key issue here, however. The fact is, that it was foolish of him to make this unnecessary vow. It could be said of Jephthah, what Solomon said in Proverbs Chapter 6.

Proverbs 6:2
> *"Thou are **snared** with the words of thy mouth, thou art **taken** with the words of thy mouth."*

When he finally realized the tremendous price involved, he was overwhelmed. Despite the agony and grief he felt, he fulfilled the vow. He **knew** a vow to God (whatever it might be), **must not be broken**.

Have you ever been *"snared with the words of your mouth"?* When it began to cost you, did you say "forget it" or:

Judges 11:35b
"I have opened my mouth to the Lord, and I cannot go back."

Again, remember:

Ecclesiastes 5:5
"Better is it that thou shouldest not vow, than that thou shouldest vow and not pay."

How I wish these truths were being taught to every couple contemplating marriage today. If they truly understood the seriousness of making vows, perhaps they would more seriously evaluate their true motives for marrying. I do not apologize for teaching these truths, because it **must be said** before another generation is lost, through **ignorance**. God expressed it well when He declared in Hosea Chapter 4.

Hosea 4:6
"My people are destroyed for lack of knowledge..."

We must declare what God has revealed in His word. **We must know** that God holds each of us **responsible** and **answerable** for our vows, **especially our marriage vows**. **The application of this truth** will be elaborated upon more fully in future chapters.

Section II

Divorce

They tell my prophets, "shut up—we don't want any more of your reports!" Or they say , "Don't tell us the truth, tell us nice things; Tell us lies. Forget all this gloom; we've heard more than enough about your 'Holy One of Israel,' and all He says.

This is the reply of the Holy One of Israel: "Because you despise what I tell you and trust instead in frauds and lies and won't repent, therefore calamity will come upon you suddenly, as upon a bulging wall that bursts and falls; in one moment it comes crashing down. God will smash you like a broken dish; he will not act sparingly. Not a piece will be left large enough to use for carrying coals from the hearth, or a little water from the well. For the Lord God, the Holy one of Israel, says: Only in returning to me and waiting for me will you be saved;... "

Isaiah 30: 10-15 (The Living Bible)

Chapter 4

The Bible and Divorce

Before we could approach this highly controversial subject, it was imperative to establish in **Section I** what the Bible had to say about:

- ☞ the **origin** of all marriages
- ☞ the **universality** of **the marriage law**
- ☞ the **seriousness** of **vows** made to God
- ☞ the **duration** of the marriage convenant.

The failure to recognize these Biblical truths has spawned a myriad of books, offering non-scriptural solutions, based upon man's past experiences and failures—not upon *"thus saith the Lord."*

I. A Biblical Premise:

The **first prerequisite** in knowing any Biblical truth, is to establish a **sound scriptural premise**. Any strong argument, if based upon a false premise, is **error**, no matter how logical or pleasant it sounds. Even if it causes a church to explode with tremendous growth, if that argument is based upon a false premise, it's still **error** and shall be judged as such by God.

II. Method of Interpretation:

It is impossible to study the subject at hand honestly, if the scriptural foundation is wrong.

While in college and seminary, I learned in my biblical hermaneutics class (the science of interpreting Scriptures), that principles of **sound Biblical interpretation** are best preserved, **when scriptural passages** which seem **unclear,** are interpreted in the light of those passages which **are clear**. If **you** will compare and evaluate Scripture with Scripture, **you** will find the Bible to be its **own best commentary**. **One rule of comparing Scripture,** that must not be disregarded, is that the **plain verses** are the **main verses**. All **obscure, and seemingly contradictory verses, must submit** to those portions which are **clear** and **concise**. In most instances, the **unclear** will be cleared up by the **clear**, and a sound verdict can be rendered.

This is basically the method of interpretation we will use in approaching this subject of marriage and divorce. We will try to compare **all** the **pertinent** Scripture portions, not just the **convenient** portions. I know that **what I believe** means **nothing** unless **all of Scripture** agrees.

I am sure that those of you who have read much on this subject, come away with the feeling that the only portions that apply today are the Laws of Moses and Matthew, Chapters 5 and 19. Most books I've read, **begin** with **the Matthew/Pauline exceptions,** and **explain away** those Scriptures that contradict those **portions**. I think, as we progress, you'll agree that the **so-called "exception Scripture passages,"** when compared to other **clear passages**, are, at best, the **unclear** or **obscure portions**.

We will approach the subject of marriage and divorce differently from most books today. We will first establish those **clear**, non-contradicting portions of Scriptures, to see if we can establish **a clear, consistent New Testament position**. Then, based upon that position, we will deal with the **unclear, obscure**, and seemingly contradictory portions. Using this approach, you will find that **there are no contradictions**. There are **no unclear** or **obscure portions**. God's Word is again **totally consistent.**

III. Clear Portions of the New Testament Concerning Divorce:

The biblical portions that establish a clear doctrinal position concerning marriage and divorce, and by which all unclear verses should be compared, are:

- ☞ Mark 10:2-12
- ☞ Luke 16:18
- ☞ Romans 7:2,3
- ☞ I Corinthians 7:39
- ☞ Hebrews 13:4
- ☞ Malachi 2:14

A. Mark 10:2-12

In approaching this section, we should **first** make note that the book of Mark was written **to the Romans** (Gentiles). Jesus was speaking in this same book to the Pharisees, whom he called *"Sons of Satan"*:

Mark 10:2-12
*"And the Pharisees came to him, and asked him, Is it lawful for a man to put away his wife? **tempting him**. And He answered and said unto them, What did Moses command you? And they said, Moses suffered to write a bill of divorcement, and to put her away. And Jesus answered and said unto them, For the hardness of your heart he wrote you this precept But **from the beginning** of the creation God made them male and female. For this cause shall a man leave his father and mother and cleave to his wife; and they twain shall be **one flesh**: so then they are no more twain, but one flesh. What*

57

therefore God hath joined together, let not man put
asunder. And in the house his disciples asked him again
*of the same matter. And he saith unto them, **whosoever***
shall put away his wife, and marry another, committeth
***adultery against her.** And if a woman shall put away*
*her husband, and be married to another, **she***
***committeth adultery**."*

Let's analyze these verses carefully, to draw out the
clearest, **most natural interpretation** possible.

First, note **who** was asking the question. The Scripture
portion already stated that it was the Pharisees.

Second, what was their **motive**? Scripture tells us they
hated the way Jesus exposed their religious sham, and
allowed them to be seen as the religious opportunists they
were.

Mark 10:2

"Is it lawful for a man to put away his wife?
tempting him."

If we can understand what Matthew meant by the
phrase, *"tempting him"* it will expose the Pharisees' motive.
They were trying to **trap Jesus!**

We have other examples of this in the Scriptures.
Matthew, Mark, and Luke recorded how the Jewish leaders
sent Pharisees and Herodians out to trap Jesus into saying
something that they could offer to the Romans as **subversive**;
to have Jesus destroyed. In Luke Chapter 20, they asked:

Luke 20:22

"Is it lawful for us to give tribute unto Caesar, or
no?"

For Jesus to answer that question, was similar to having someone today ask you if you have **stopped** beating your wife, or **stopped** cheating on your husband. You can't answer those questions either way without getting into trouble with someone. The same was true here; "**yes**" or "**no**" was not sufficient.

Their purpose, was to **either** get the Romans after Him for insurrection, or the Jewish zealots angry with him for agreeing to pay taxes to Rome. These zealots felt no taxes should be paid. Jesus, however said:

> **Luke 20:24 (The Living Bible)**
> *"Show me a coin."*

When they did, he responded:

> **Luke 20:24 (The Living Bible)**
> *"Whose portrait is this on it? And whose name?"*

They replied:

> *"Caesar's."*

Jesus answered:

> **Luke 20:25 (The Living Bible)**
> *"Then give the emperor all that is his—and give God all that is his!"*

Verse 26 is beautiful:

> **Luke 20:26 (The Living Bible)**
> *"Thus their attempt to outwit him before the people failed ; and marveling at his answer, they were silent."*

Jesus eluded the trap they had set to destroy Him.

Just as the Pharisees tried to **trap** Jesus in Luke Chapter 20, they likewise tried again in Mark Chapter 10. It is imperative that we **know this background** to understand Christ's answer.

1. Liberal or Conservative?

The Pharisees asked Jesus, *"...Is it lawful for a man to put away his wife?"* They were again playing **partisan politics**. Just as we have a political and religious "left" and "right" today, which are sometimes called "liberal" and "conservative," so did the Jewish people, in Christ's day. There were **two mainline religious interpretations** being taught in Jesus' day concerning Deuteronomy 24.

Deuteronomy 24: 1-4
"When a man hath taken a wife, and married her, and it come to pass that she find no favour in his eyes, because he hath found some uncleanness in her: then let him write her a bill of divorcement...and send her out of his house."

These two well-known interpretations were constantly being debated among the Rabbis. These Rabbinical schools, as they were called, each with its own interpretation, were named after their founders.

The liberal interpretation was set forth by **Rabbi Hillel**. To Hillel, that portion of Deuteronomy, meant that if a man were married, and his wife embarrassed him before his parents, yelled at him, danced in public with her hair down, burned the bagels, or if he just found a prettier girl, **these** would be **grounds for**

60

divorce, with the option to marry someone else. Today we call it "**incompatibility**."

On the other hand, if the wife found her husband was leprous, tumorous, a heretic, or was engaged in a dirty trade, such as a tanner or coppersmith; and it became unbearable, these would be grounds for divorce, and she would be free to marry someone else.

The "**conservative position**," was set forth by **Rabbi Shammai**. Shammai said that divorce was possible **only** in the case of **unchastity**. **Only moral uncleanness** constituted grounds for divorce and marriage to a second partner. **Today** we would call that "**prevailing Christian theology**."

Keep in mind these two positions as you note Jesus' answer. He could have very easily said: "I agree with Rabbi Hillel, or I agree with Rabbi Shammai," and settled the whole issue then and there.

If you read the prevailing theories, concerning marriage and divorce, available today, in books found in most of our Christian bookstores, it becomes clear, that **the Shammai doctrine** is with us. To even **dare suggest another possible doctrinal position,** is received by the majority of churches today, as **tantamount to heresy**. If the Shammai teaching **were true,** then Jesus totally and tragically missed this choice opportunity to endorse it.

2. Our Lord's Response

Please note how Jesus responded to these Pharisees. He **ignored Hillel and Shammai** as though they didn't exist. You see, Jesus never was overly impressed with **the prevalent interpretations** that were in vogue in His day. He called them "*traditions.*"

Mark 7:6-9

"...*Well hath Esaias prophesied of **you hypocrites**, as it is written, This people honoureth me with their lips, but their heart is far from me. Howbeit **in vain** do they worship me, **teaching for doctrines the commandments of men**. For **laying aside the commandment of God**, ye **hold the tradition of men**, as the washing of pots and cups: and many other such like things ye do. **And he said unto them**,* (Watch this now; here you get **Christ's attitude toward the traditions** of Shammai and Hillel.) ***full well ye reject the commandment of God**, that ye may keep **your own tradition**.*"

Mark 7:9 (The Living Bible)

"*You are simply **rejecting God's laws** and trampling them under your feet for the sake of **tradition**.*"

The traditions of Christ's day, were arrived at, by the same process as our present day laws have evolved. Our founding fathers established our Constitution, but then the Judicial Branch of our government began to interpret it. One said, "In my opinion, it means this." Then another got hold of that interpretation of the law, and interpreted the interpretation. Along came another lawmaker, who interpreted the interpretation, of the interpretation, of the original law. Now you multiply that cycle many times over, and you'll see why today, black is white, down is up, evil is good, and wrong is right. You'll understand why in some states, a twelve-year old girl **can't** get her ears pierced without her parents' permission, but **can** get an abortion, without parental consent. One could go on ad nauseam with the perverted, distorted revisions of good laws, that have become meaningless **traditions of men**. The teachings of Shammai and Hillel, were what was left of **God's true standard of marriage,** after the religious leaders got through with them.

3. Dangers of Traditions

In Matthew Chapter 23, Jesus rebuked the religious leaders for this very practice.

Matthew 23:23-25

"Woe unto you, scribes and Pharisees, hypocrites! for ye pay tithes of mint and anise and cummin, and have omitted the weightier matters of **the law***, judgment, mercy, and faith: these ought ye to have done, and not to leave the other undone. Ye blind guides, which strain at a gnat and swallow a camel. Woe unto you, scribes and Pharisees, hypocrites! for ye* **make clean the outside of the cup and of the platter, but within** *they are* **full** *of* **extortion** *and* **excess.***"*

Paul the Apostle warns against this danger today—The danger of replacing what Jesus taught, with the traditions of men.

Colossians 2:6-8

"As ye have therefore received Christ Jesus **the Lord***, so walk ye in him: Rooted and built up* **in Him***, and stablished in the faith,* **as ye have been taught***, abounding therein with thanksgiving.* **Beware***, lest any man spoil you through philosophy and vain deceit, after* **the tradition of men***, after the* **rudiments** *of the world, and* **not after Christ.** *"*

Colossians 2:8b (The Living Bible)

*"Their **wrong** and **shallow** answers **built on men's thoughts** and **ideas**, instead of on what Christ has said."*

Herein lies one of **the greatest dangers** in the Church today. Many God-fearing pastors, pressed beyond the limit by their schedules, yet sensing the urgency of this divorce problem in the Church, desperately seek out **what other men say**. The result is philosophies *"built on men's thoughts and ideas."*

Jesus **totally ignored** and disregarded Shammai and Hillel's teachings for what they were. They were *"men's teachings."* that were **contrary** to what God had declared. This should give us an idea of how valuable our most important theories are in God's eyes, if they are not based upon, and consistent with His Word.

4. Seeking for an Authority

Jesus answered the Pharisees, in Mark Chapter 10, by going back to **the one authority** they recognized. The **one man's writings** upon which all their laws were based, before the so-called **thinkers or authorities** got hold of them.

Mark 10:3-5

*"...What did **Moses** command you? And they said, **Moses suffered to write** a bill of divorcement, and to put her away. And Jesus answered and said unto them, **for the hardness of your heart he** (Moses-**he**, not God) **wrote you** (hard-hearted, Mark 10:5 stiffnecked Jews) **this precept."***

Jesus was showing that during Moses's time of leadership, Moses **initiated** a **special situation or dispensation,** to accommodate the **rebellious circumstances** he encountered, when dealing with Israel. This was not the norm; it was an accommodation, a compromise, an allowance.

Mark 10:5

*"...For the **hardness of your hearts,** he* (**Moses**) *wrote you this precept. "*

It was a matter of **sufferance** because after several hundred years in Egypt, their concept of God was so low.

W. W. Davies in his article on "Divorce in the Old Testament" in the **International Standard Bible Encyclopedia** (Vol. II, Pages 863-864) says:

> **"Moses' aim was to regulate and thus to mitigate an evil which he could not extirpate...The Mosaic law apparently, on the side of the husband, made it as difficult as possible for him to secure a divorce."[3]**

It's interesting to note, that the Mosaic bill of divorcement, **was never applicable in the case of adultery**. It wasn't applicable, because the adulterer was **stoned to death**.

Again, I quote W. W. Davies from the same passage on page 864.

---

[3] Quotes from International Standard Bible Encyclopedia: Copyright 1939 Wm. B. Eerdmans Publishing Co., Grand Rapids, Michigan. Used by permission.

"We know of no modern version which makes...(*'some uncleanness'* in the Hebrew)...the equivalent of fornication or adultery. And, indeed, in the very nature of the case we are forced to make the words apply to a minor fault or crime, for, by the Mosaic law, the penalty for adultery was death. (Dt 22:20 ff)"[4]

The writing of a bill of divorcement, was **for other reasons**, but **never** for adultery. **Adultery has never been grounds for divorce in the Bible.** Grounds for the **death penalty— yes**—but **never grounds for divorce.** Once you settle this fact in your mind, the other answers will come easier. Let me state that again.

Adultery has never been grounds for divorce in the Bible. This is why Moses commanded, that if they insisted on putting away their wives, that they give, in writing, **the true reason**, so evil reports could not circulate about the wife. You must realize as you read, **whatever Moses allowed the nation of Israel to do**, it was an accommodation, and contrary to God's original design, as found in Genesis 2:22-24.

In Exodus Chapter 32, **God's solution to Moses was clear.** While Moses had been on the Mount receiving the Decalogue, the nation of Israel had Aaron make a golden calf for them. When Moses came down, Israel was worshipping the calf and having a paganistic celebration. Then, God said to Moses, in Exodus Chapter 32:

---

[4] Quotes from International Standard Bible Encyclopedia: Copyright 1939 Wm. B. Eerdmans Publishing Co., Grand Rapids, Michigan. Used by permission.

Exodus 32:9-10

"...I have seen this people, and, behold, it is a stiffnecked people: Now therefore let me alone, that my wrath may wax hot against them, and that I may consume them: (wipe them all out) ***And I will make of thee a great nation.***" (I'll start all over again. These people are so hardhearted, and stiffnecked; it would be easier to start over.) (Paraphrased)

If Moses hadn't interceded, the history of Israel would have been drastically altered that day. After this, **all future dealings** with Israel by Moses, **had to be**, if I may use the term again, an accommodation, contrary to God's original design. Jesus was saying, "Don't think what Moses did was God's way, it was **introduced only** because **our forefathers couldn't be ruled and regulated**." (We will expound more on this truth in Chapter 6.)

Jesus' next words in Matthew Chapter 19 were:

Matthew 19:8

*"Moses because of the hardness of your hearts suffered you to put away your wives...**but,*** (**note this! Here is the pivot point. Moses did** what he did because of your hard hearts, because of **extenuating circumstances**.) ***But from*** (**not, but at**), ***but from the beginning it was not so.***"

Jesus **ignored** Hillel and Shammai; He clarified the **carnal foundation** upon which Moses had allowed or commanded the writing of the bill of divorcement. Now, **He goes back beyond Moses, to the origin**.

Jesus went all the way back to **God's eternal standard—God's universal marriage law**. The word *"from"* is interesting here.

Matthew 19:8

"But from the beginning it was not so..."

In the Greek, the word *"from,"* is written in the perfect tense. If Jesus had said *"at—the beginning,"* it could have meant something entirely different; but He said *"from."* The perfect tense indicates **a continuing action, that has never ceased.** This is vital to see if we are to understand what Jesus is saying here. He's saying (paraphrase): "I don't care what Shammai and Hillel say. I know the extenuating circumstances under which Moses wrote our fathers the divorce precept. But here's what you Pharisees need to know—it was **never God's intention—*'from the beginning'* until now, and from now on**. Here is God's universal law, **unchanged**. I am **reaffirming** it now, for it has **never changed**."

Mark 10:6-8

"...from the beginning of the creation God made them male and female. for this cause shall a man (any man) *leave his father and mother, and cleave to his wife; and they twain shall be one flesh: so then they are no more twain, but one flesh."*

Does this sound familiar? Jesus said what His Father said at the beginning—**not** what Moses said—**not** what Hillel and Shammai said—**but** what **his Father said.**

Mark 10:9

"What therefore... " (**therefore**—What's it there for? It's there because Jesus just **reaffirmed divine truth,** by which all mankind is to live today.) *"What therefore **God hath joined** together, let not man put asunder."*

The Living Bible says:
"...No man may separate (divorce) *what God has joined together."*

We're getting close to some powerful, irrefutable statements, made by our Lord Jesus Christ, that we **don't dare miss!**

In Mark 10:10-11

*"And in the house his disciples asked him again of the same matter. And He saith **unto them...** "*

Up to now, Jesus was speaking to **blind Pharisees.** But **now,** He's **teaching divine truth, to the future church. He is building a doctrinal basis, upon which the church may function. Whatever** Jesus says here, we can accept as **New Testament truth.** This is **not legalism.** This is **not condemnation.** This is not the **"letter of the law that killeth."** Rather, it is our Lord **reestablishing to the church,** that truth, which sin, hardheartedness, religiosity, compromise and Satan, have been trying to steal from it.

Notice verse 11:
"and He (Jesus) *saith unto them,* (the disciples) *whosoever."*

What does *"whosoever"* mean? Let's compare the same word in other verses.

John 3:16
   *"...**whosoever** believeth in Him should not perish..."*

Does that mean **some** who believe in Him, or **all** who believe in Him? **All**, of course = **whosoever means everyone**.

John 8:34
   *"...**whosoever** committeth sin is the servant of sin."*

Does that mean **some** who commit sin are the servants of sin, or **all** who commit sin are the servants of sin—**all**, of course.

In every instance, it includes **all persons** in that category. Here again, Jesus is confirming, that the **divine marriage law,** is a **universal law**, and not applicable just to born again Christians. When Jesus said in Mark 10:11, *"**whosoever...**"* that is **a universal term,** including **everyone** in this particular category, **saved, and unsaved alike**. What group of people is Jesus speaking of here?

Mark 10:11
   *"...**Whosoever** shall put away his wife."*

He's speaking of **every married** person.

Next:
   *"Whosoever shall **put away** his wife ..."*

The Greek word for *"put away"* is "Apoluo," meaning "to loose or put away."

Finis Jennings Dake in the Dake's Annotated Bible notes, in a parallel passage (Matthew 5:31 Note "e") says:

> **"Put away means 'divorce' and was so understood by the Jews ..."**[5]

Therefore, Jesus is saying,

> **"any man** who is married and **divorces** his wife."

Now watch this!

> *"And marry another, committeth adultery against her."* Against his wife.

No qualification! No exceptions! I know that Matthew 5 and 19 give a qualification, but our **purpose** here, is **to first establish a consistent Biblical premise** with the **clear** verses, and then, test the **unclear** passages, in the light of the **clear.** We will deal with **the Matthew exceptions** later on in the book.

For now though, Jesus Himself gave **no exceptions** in the Gospel of Mark, which was written basically to the Romans (Gentiles). In verse 12, He reverses the order, but establishes the same truth, when He says:

Mark 10:12

> *"And if a* **woman** (any woman) *shall put away* (divorce) *her husband, and be married to another she* **committeth adultery."**

---

[5]Dake's Annotated Reference Bible by Finis Jennings Drake, Dake Bible Sales, Lawrenceville, GA. Used by Permission.

Here it is again, **without exceptions**.

It is important to **visualize** what Jesus actually said here to show His **premise or basis of argument**.

Here are Jack and Jill, as two individuals. Refer to Illustration #3.

Illustration #3

Jack   **Jill**

Two separate, single individuals.

When Jack and Jill marry, they look like this to God. Refer to Illustration #4.

Illustration #4

Jack   **Jill**

(One Flesh)
Till Death

Upon taking their **vows**, God made them *"one flesh."*

Jesus says, if Jack divorces Jill … (Refer to Illustration #5)

Illustration #5

Legally divorced by society.

"**And marries another**," (Refer to Illustration #6)

Illustration #6

Legally married by society, but Jesus called it **adultery**,
"and marries again, commits adultery."

Jesus says, **Jack** is committing **adultery against Jill**.

How is that **possible**? Didn't Jesus say Jack **divorced** her? Whatever the reason, if he divorced Jill, how could he be **committing adultery**? Notice what Jesus said.

Mark 10:8
> *"They are no more* (or **never** again) *twain, but one flesh."*

Notice in Illustration #6, how Jack's edge, does not fit with Sue's edge? Do you see that if Jill were placed next to Jack again, that they **still fit**? This is what Jesus was saying to the disciples, **"I don't recognize men's divorce."** You and I **cannot destroy** with a **piece of legal paper** or **immoral sin**, what God has **supernaturally** created— *"one flesh"* **for life**. Even though Jack went through the **legal motions** of an earthly divorce, and he and Sue experienced a **socially legal** marriage ceremony, Jesus said, **"in God's sight** it is an **adulterous relationship."**

Mark 10:11b
> *"whosoever shall put away* (divorce) *his wife,* (or husband) *and marry another, committeth adultery against her."*

Adultery, is a **sex relationship outside a marriage union**. Jesus said, the husband and/or wife **divorced** the other, **but**, in marrying another person, they **both** were **committing adultery against the other**. That's **impossible,** unless Jesus was saying that He **did not recognize divorce**.

74

It was simply stated, in Mark Chapter 10, that **Jesus totally ignored local popular tradition**. **He explained, and qualified, the concessionary nature** of Moses' *"writing of divorcement."* He also **re-established** the universal nature and jurisdiction of the divine law, of the *"one flesh"* concept of marriage. He accomplished this, by **refusing** to recognize divorce, **for any cause**.

B. Luke 16:18

Now, let's look at **Luke 16:18**. It contains a very short, concise statement. Luke was written, basically **to the Greeks,** concerning Christ. Let's see if Mark and Luke agree.

Luke 16:18

*"Whosoever putteth away his wife, and marrieth another, **committeth adultery**: and whosoever marrieth her that is put away from her husband, **committeth adultery.**"*

This verse **totally agrees** with what Jesus said in Mark. Jack divorces Jill, for whatever the reason, and marries Sue. God calls it **adultery**. He **cannot** recognize the **second vows,** because **he has already acted** upon the **first** vows, and made Jack and Jill *"one flesh **for life.**"*

Please note however, that Luke 16:18 goes **one step further**. Remember, **Jesus said it**, and we're only repeating what He said. We're not **adding to,** or **taking away, interpreting**, or trying to create **our own thesis**. We don't **need** to **interpret** anything here; it is **self-explanatory**. Jesus went further by saying:

Luke 16:18b

"and whosoever marrieth her that is put away from her husband committeth adultery."

Let's visualize that:

Jack divorces Jill and marries Sue. Jesus said that is *"adultery."* Refer to Illustration #7 .

Illustration #7

Legally married by society
Jesus called it "adultery"

Now, Jesus says that if **Sam** marries Jill (the **innocent party**) **he** is an **adulterer** also. Read it again for yourself.

Luke 16:18

"*Whosoever,* (**universal, no exception**) *marrieth her* (Jill) *that is put away from her husband* (divorced by Jack, who has already married Sue), *committeth adultery.*" Refer to Illustration #8.

Illustration #8

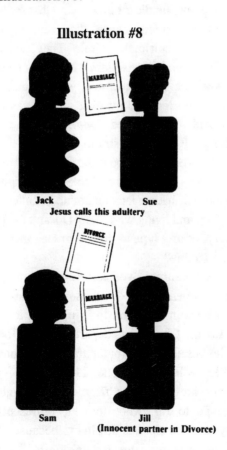

Jack   Sue
Jesus calls this adultery

Sam   Jill
(Innocent partner in Divorce)

Jesus calls this adultery.

He was declaring that Jack and Jill were still *"one flesh,"* **regardless of man's laws.**

We must **see,** what Jesus is teaching here, to **His disciples.** When Jack and Jill came as **two single persons,** (neither having been married before) and **pledged** themselves to each other, **God's divine, universal marriage law** went into effect; and they were made *"one flesh,"* by a **supernatural act of God.** Remember, **people marry people,** but only God can make two *"one flesh,"* for life. Therefore, when Jack **thought** he was divorcing Jill and marrying Sue, **he didn't** understand that something happened **beyond the signed license,** that went beyond the physical and into the spiritual realm. They, Jack and Jill, **had already become** *"one flesh"* **in God's sight** for **life.**

After Jack, **in ignorance,** went through the **civil act** of divorce, and **legally,** by man's law, was married to Sue, Jesus said it constituted *"adultery."* Jack **was living in adultery.** Refer to Illustration #8.

Jill, who would today be described as "**the innocent party,**" **was civilly** married to Sam. Again see Illustration #8. After all, hadn't Jack committed adultery against her, by marrying, and living with Sue? Doesn't **everyone know** that adultery, or **any type of moral uncleanness,** is **grounds for divorce today?**

It's **Shammai over Jesus**—traditions of men **over** the **commandments** of God. Please understand, I'm not putting these things in this book **to injure,** but to cause you to see **how far** the Church has departed from God's Word.

Jesus said to Sam (paraphrased), "I **know** Jack divorced Jill; I **know** he married Sue. **That's adultery,** because Jack and Jill are **still** *'one flesh'* in My sight. Now your **marriage** to Jill, who, to you, represents **the innocent party,** also constitutes **adultery,** because; *'They* (Jack and Jill) *are no more twain, but one flesh.'*"

Society accepts remarriage as the norm, but Jesus says it is **adultery**. Therefore, Mark 10 and Luke 16 agree completely.

Let's check with Paul now.

C. Romans 7:2-3

Romans 7:2-3

*"For the woman which hath an husband is **bound by the law** (The marriage law) to her husband so **long as he liveth**; but if the husband be dead, she is **loosed** from the law of her husband. So then, if, while her husband liveth, she be married to another man, **she shall be called an adulteress**: but if her husband **be dead**, she is free from that law; so that she is no adulteress, though she be married to another man,"*

I have read this portion to grade school children and said, "Please tell me what this is saying." Their response has always been clear, "The Bible says **married people are married for life**." Now I wonder, **if children** can see that, **why can't adults**? Perhaps its because the children do not look at this portion of Scripture with preconceived ideas. This portion **totally agrees with Mark and Luke** and is unequivocally clear; **marriage is for life**. Can you see a **clear scriptural premise** forming?

You might now ask, "Why can't Jack and Sue or Sam and Jill be *"one flesh"* if they made **the same vows** that Jack and Jill made previously? **Weren't their vows just as binding?"** No! The very exclusive nature of Jack and Jill's **first vows before God, automatically invalidated Jack's vows to Sue, and Jill's vows to Sam.** In other words, if the first ones are to be accepted and honored as valid, then they will, by their very nature and content, **invalidate the second**.

Let me illustrate what Jesus was saying. If you and I were close friends and I came to you and said, "I don't have many possessions in this life, but I do have one new car—a fully equipped Cadillac. I love you so much that **I want you to have it**. Here is the title, signed and notarized, transferring it to you; and here are the keys. It's yours! **You** now are the proud owner of a brand new Cadillac."

In a few weeks, you receive the title for the new Cadillac from the state, with your name on it, and you begin to enjoy **your new car**. A couple of weeks later, someone walks up to you and says, "I was just talking to Joe Webb, and he said to me, 'I don't have many possessions in this life, but I do have one new car—a fully equipped Cadillac. I love you so much that **I want you to have it**.' Joe said you were driving the car, and I was supposed to come and get it."

What would you say about that? You'd probably say, "**So sorry!** Joe has **no more say** over the disposition of this car. He gave it to me, and **it's mine**. He **no longer** has **any authority or rights** over this car. It's **no longer his to give**."

In like manner, when one gives himself or herself to another in marriage, he/she **loses, or forfeits the freedom** to give his/her body to another, because he/she has become *"one flesh"* with that partner for life, and is seen as one person in God's sight, *"till death."*

I Corinthians 7:3-5 says:

*"Let the husband render unto the wife due benevolence: and likewise also the wife unto the husband. **the wife hath not power of her own body, but the husband: and likewise also the husband hath not power of his own body**, but the wife. Defraud ye*

80

not one the other, except it be with consent for a time, that ye may give yourselves to fasting and prayer; and come together again, that Satan tempt you not for your incontinency."

Note how The Living Bible says it:

*"The man should give his wife all that is her right as a married woman, and the wife should do the same for her husband: for a girl who marries **no longer has full right to her own body**, for her husband then has his rights to it too: and in the same way the husband **no longer has full right to his own body**, for it belongs also to his wife. So do not refuse these rights to each other. **The only exception to this rule** would be the agreement of both husband and wife to refrain from the rights of marriage for a limited time, so that they can give themselves more completely to prayer. Afterwards, they should come together again so that Satan won't be able to tempt them because of their lack of self-control."*

God's Word says that when you made the **original marriage vow**, you **signed the title** of the ownership of your body to your first partner **for life**. Therefore, even if Jack and Jill divorce, and declare vows over again with Sue and Sam, they no longer have **the title** to transfer. Jill **owns** Jack's body and Jack **owns** Jill's body, and that ownership **is for life**. Since God **confirmed** the **original vows**, He would **deny** His own holiness and righteousness to **recognize** the second. Therefore Jesus said in Luke Chapter 16:

Luke 16:18

*"Whosoever putteth away his wife and marrieth another, **committeth adultery**; and whosoever marrieth her that is put away from her husband **committeth adultery**."*

He was saying, "**I cannot accept** those vows, for you **no longer** have **legal title** to give yourself to another, until one or the other dies."

Thus, in the case of **Sam and Sue**, if each were **previously unmarried**, they are **still unmarried in God's sight,** because they **could not** become *"one flesh"* with Jack or Jill, because Jack and Jill will be *"one flesh,"* until one or the other dies.

If Sam or Sue were previously married and divorced, before declaring vows, they are **still married** to their **former partners,** and **do not have a legal title** to transfer the ownership of **their** bodies to another, until their first partner dies, and they are released from their **original vows.** Paul states this in I Corinthians Chapter 7.

I Corinthians 7:10-11, 39

*"And unto the married I command, yet **not I but the Lord** ..."*

Paul says, (Paraphrased.)

("What I'm about to tell you is totally consistent with what our Lord Jesus Christ taught. In fact, He **commanded me to tell you this, as a command!** Whatever it is, **it's mandatory**.") *"Let **not the wife depart** (this Greek word means **to separate**—not divorce) from her husband, but... "*

Here's that **pivot point** again. She's not supposed to leave for just any reason whatsoever. *"but"* The Lord is **practical,** and knows **some conditions** can be **ubearable**. One's husband or wife may leave, and the other spouse would have no control over that situation. One spouse may be cruel or brutal to the rest of the family, and create an atmosphere of danger for them. Consequently, God had made provision in his Word, to provide an answer for such situations. **Here is God's only scriptural provision** for seemingly impossible marriage situations: to separate, remain single, or reconcile. This is **Scripture's** only **out,** other than death.

> **I Corinthians 7:11**
> *"But and if she depart, let her remain unmarried* (never let anyone tell you that these are grounds for marrying someone else) *let her remain unmarried or be reconciled to her husband: and let not the husband put away* (divorce) *his wife."*

God's Word is in **full agreement** concerning *"one flesh"* relationships for life.

D. I Corinthians 7:39

> **I Corinthians 7:39**
> *"The wife is bound by the law as long as her husband liveth: but if her husband be dead, she is at liberty to be married to whom she will; only in the Lord."*

This portion is **written to Christians specifically,** but is **totally consistent** with all the other universally aimed Scripture portions so far. Paul established that **true saints** are those who have **repented of their past,** and are living changed lives.

> **Ephesians 5:1-8**
> *"Be ye therefore followers (imitators) of God, as dear children; and walk in love, as Christ also hath loved us, and hath given Himself for us an offering and a sacrifice to God for a sweetsmelling savour. But fornication, and all uncleanness, or covetousness, let it not be once named among you, as becometh saints;*

Neither filthiness, nor foolish talking, nor jesting, which are not convenient: but rather giving of thanks. For this ye know, that no whoremonger, nor unclean person, nor covetous man, who is an idolater, hath any inheritance in the kingdom of Christ and of God.

*Let **no man deceive you with vain words**: for **because of these things** cometh the wrath of God upon the children of disobedience. Be not ye therefore partakers with them. For ye were sometimes darkness, but now are ye light in the Lord: **walk as children of light**:"*

Here we sense **the seriousness** of these things being allowed in the Church today. Paul warns us not to be deceived on these matters. Whenever the Word of God says, **"Be Not Deceived,"** you can be sure that's an area where we have to be careful, or **we will be deceived**.

E. Hebrews 13:4

Hebrews 13:4
*"Marriage is honourable in all, and the bed undefiled: but **whoremongers, and adulterers** God will judge."*

Note: The word **"whoremonger"** in this portion of Scripture is **"pornos,"** in the Greek, which can also be translated, **"fornicator."** Clear—concise—and it is in **total agreement** with the portions of Scripture already mentioned.

F. Malachi 2:14-16a

In **Malachi 2,** God was speaking to the Jews concerning their backsliding and indifference. He indicated it had come to the place where He would no longer listen to their prayers and offerings.

Malachi 2:14 -16a (The Amplified Bible)
"You ask, why does He reject it." [the sacrificial offerings—they were offering them to God **with tears**]

The Living Bible says:
"Why has God abandoned us?"

The Amplified Bible states (Verse 14-16a)
*"Because the Lord was **witness to the covenant** [made at your marriage] between you and the wife of your youth, against whom you have dealt treacherously and to whom you were faithless. Yet she is **your companion**, and **the wife of your covenant [made by your marriage vows]**. And did not **God make you** and your wife **one flesh**? Did not God make you one and preserve your spirit alive? And **why did God make you two one**? Because **He sought a godly offspring** from your union. Therefore take heed to yourselves, and **let no one** deal treacherously and be faithless to the wife of his youth; For the Lord God of Israel says: **I hate divorce and marital separation**,"*

IV. Conclusion:

We now have a premise upon which to **build a doctrine** from the Scripture, and to **test** the **unclear passages**. This should help us establish **a sound biblical interpretation**. We can now repeat **the definition of marriage,** based upon the verses dealt with so far.

"Marriage is a process of divine origin and regulation, by which any man and woman, by mutual consent, are

united by God, for the purpose of living together permanently in love, in order to establish and maintain a home and family."

V. A Review:

A. Marriage was established, and the marriage law is universally regulated by God.

B. The marriage law is binding for life.

C. The marriage law is activated by mutual vows.

D. How God view's divorce:

    1. A clear consistent biblical premise.

        a. Mark 10:2-12

        b. Luke 16:18

        c. Romans 7:2,3

        d. I Corinthians 7:10-11,39

        e. Hebrews 13:4

        f. Malachi 2:16

    2. To marry another after divorce constitutes adultery.

    3. Any persons who have married again after divorce while their first spouse still lives, are adulterers.

    4. Unrepentant adulterers shall be judged by God.

I am sure some of you are saying, "If this is true, why haven't we heard of it in our schools of theology, or our pulpits?" To answer this question, it is necessary for us to examine the teachings of the early church, and find out where and how error entered in.

*F*or Herod himself had sent forth and laid hold upon John (the Baptist) and bound him in prison for Herodias' sake, his brother Phillip's wife: for he had married her. For John had said unto Herod, It is not lawful for thee to have thy brother's wife.

Mark 6:17-18

*W*hosoever putteth away his wife, and marrieth another, committeth adultery: and whosoever marrieth her that is put away from her husband committeth adultery.

Luke 16:18

Chapter 5

Early Church Positions

In this section, thus far we have considered:

☞ The clear biblical verses that establish a consistent doctrinal premise.

Many Christian leaders today, who are historically Evangelical, Fundamental, Bible-believing, New Testament, or Orthodox in their doctrine, are unknowingly preaching a non-Biblical, **humanistic substitute,** that was introduced into the church in the sixteenth century.

Historically, there have been **five basic theological positions** on marriage and divorce in the Christian church since the first century. William A. Heth and Gordon J. Wenham teach extensively on these in their book, <u>**Jesus and Divorce**</u>, published by Thomas Nelson Publishers. Paul Steele and Charles Ryrie, in their book, <u>**Meant To Last**</u>, published by Victor Books, also describe these positions in detail. (Both of these books are presently out of print.)

The first four of these oldest Church positions, are:
1. **The Patristic View** (or Early Father's View)
2. **The Preteritive View** (or Augustinian View)

3. **The Betrothal View** (or Engagement View)
4. **The Consanguinity View** (or Unlawful Marriage View)[6]

All four of these earliest church views conclude that the Bible teaches that marriage is **for life**, and to divorce and marry another person, while the first spouse is still living, **is forbidden**, and constitutes adultery.

Steele and Ryrie also said,

> **"Careful research through the hundreds of manuscripts written by church leaders of the first five centuries has revealed that with only one exception (Ambrosiaster, a fourth century Latin writer) the Church Fathers were unanimous in their understanding that Christ and Paul taught that if one were to suffer the misfortune of divorce, remarriage was not permitted, regardless of the cause. This remained the standard view of the Church until the sixteenth century when Erasmus, suggested a different idea that was taken over by protestant theologians."[7]**

5. **The Historic View/Erasmian View**

The fifth **historic** view, not written until the 16th century, is called **the Erasmian View,** (or Traditional Protestant View). It teaches that the **innocent party** is allowed to **divorce, and** subsequently **permitted to marry** another, in the case of **adultery**, desertion, or any *"moral uncleanness."* **Today** this

---

[6] Steele Paul E. and Ryrie Charles C., <u>Meant to Last</u> (Wheaton, Illinois, Victor Books, 1983), pp. 88, 89. (out of print)

[7] Steele, Paul E. and Ryrie, Charles C., <u>Meant to Last</u> (Wheaton, Illinois, Victor Books, 1983), 1983, pp. 88, 89. (out of print)

view is called **the Matthew and Pauline Exception Theory, or the Traditional Protestant View.**

Disiderius Erasmus (1467-1536), after whom this doctrine was named, was otherwise known as Erasmus of Rotterdam. Today he is recognized in our university libraries, as **the Prince of Humanists**. This same man was **declared a heretic** by the early Roman Church, and most of his writings were banned or burned.

Erasmus, translated the Latin New Testament into English, and at first welcomed and encouraged the Reformation. When Luther studied Erasmus' writings, he adopted some of his positions, but eventually disfellowshipped Erasmus, and declared him to be **a skeptic and a rationalist**. The Protestant Reformation occurred under the leadership of Martin Luther, who declared justification was by faith alone.

Later, Luther learned the truth about this very intelligent and talented man's aberrant lifestyle. Upon Erasmus' death, Luther said:

> **"He did so (died) without light and without the cross...I curse Erasmus, and all who think contrary to the Word...Erasmus is worthy of great hatred...I warn you to regard him as God's enemy...He inflames the baser passions of young boys, and regards Christ as I regard Klaus Nerr (the court fool)."[8]**

In his treatise, Erasmus introduced the idea that any marriage was capable of being dissolved. It seemed monstrously cruel to him that a couple should be compelled to stay together in the flesh, when they no longer, and perhaps never were, united in their spirits. In his notes on the New Testament, he introduced long excuses for divorce, from such texts as I Corinthians 7, and Matthew 5 and 19, saying that Jesus approved of divorce, due to

---

[8] Smith, Preserved, Erasmus, A Study of His Life, Ideals, and Place in History (New York: Frederick Unger Publishing Col., 1962).

the hardheartedness of the people, and that those whose marriages are already on the rocks, should be granted divorces, and be permitted to marry again. These were his conclusions, regardless of what the other, clear Scripture verses taught.

After establishing these false premises, which were **totally contrary** to early church theology, other reformers added more false reasonings to this corrupt premise, applying **Deuteronomy 24:1-4** as proof of **divine approval** for divorce, and the right to marry again.

The question I would ask is, "Whom will we believe? Will we believe Erasmus, the immoral humanistic heretic, whose teaching on marriage and divorce contradicts **all** the **teachings of our early Christian fathers**, and flies in the face of what Paul and Jesus Christ clearly taught? Or will we believe the Apostle Paul and our Lord Jesus Christ himself?"

Remember that **any doctrine,** built upon a **false premise** is a **false doctrine**, and causes those who receive it, to move from a scriptural answer, to *"their own misguided ideas."* **(II Timothy 4:4**, The Living Bible)

This **false Erasmian** doctrine, it must be remembered, was only **one of five historic positions. Many reformationists,** and present day theologians, have **ignored** the other **four earlier positions completely,** and embraced the **Erasmian view**. In so doing, they are causing to be fulfilled, the very scene which Jesus described, concerning the **last days**.

Matthew 24:37-38

> *"But as the days of Noah were...they were marrying and giving in marriage."*

This perfectly describes most churches today.

If you desire, you can read more about the teachings of Erasmus, whom his contemporary, Martin Luther, cursed, and declared to be an **enemy of God**. To learn more of this man Erasmus, who **wrote** the **Matthew and Pauline Exception**

Theology, legitimatizing divorce and the right to marry again, all you need to do is go to the **public library,** and find books about, or by, this **Prince of Humanists.** The real tragedy is that you can go to almost any **Christian book store,** and find his teachings and philosophy **permeating** a majority of the books in the Family section, concerning **marriage** and **divorce,** written by **evangelical Christian authors!**

Church leaders who preach that we must **stop humanism** in our schools and government, are, by preaching the **Erasmian View,** teaching pure, undiluted **humanism** from their **pulpits!**

Chapter 6

Biblical Exceptions —
Real or Imagined?

Building upon:

☞ A clear biblical premise.
☞ A clear understanding of where humanistic error entered into church doctrine.

We can now examine the unclear portions of Scripture, that have been used, to so vehemently excuse non-biblical lifestyles today.

With **a clear, consistent premise** from which to operate, let's **carefully and honestly approach** what are described as "**the exception verses.**" Are they **really** an **exception** to what we've learned so far, and **contradictory** to it, or will they **harmonize perfectly**? We know God's Word **does not contradict** itself; so therefore, whatever truth we find here, will **have to agree perfectly** with what we've already discussed. But **how** is this possible?

The portions in question are:

☞ **Matthew 5:27-32**
☞ **Matthew 19:5-12**
☞ **I Corinthians 7:12-16**

The Matthew 5 portion, was spoken to the **disciples**. The Matthew 19 portion, was spoken to the **pharisees**, and the Corinthians portion, was written to the **church of Corinth**.

95

Matthew - Written to Jews:

It's important to note also, that most scholars agree that Matthew was uniquely written to the Jews, to prove that Jesus Christ was really **the "Promised One"**—the Messiah. I have listed for you three proofs, as evidence to this fact.

Proof # 1

We find in Matthew, and **only** in Matthew, a lineage of both Mary and Joseph, to prove to the Jews, that **no other person** but Jesus Christ, could qualify as the promised Messiah.

Proof # 2

Whereas Mark and Luke make many references to *"the Kingdom of God;"* Matthew is different. Since the Jews were looking for an **earthly kingdom**, they couldn't understand why Jesus said the following:

> **John 18:36**
> *"My kingdom is not of this world..."*

In the book of Matthew, instead of using the same phrase as was used in Mark and Luke, i.e., *"The Kingdom of God,"* Jesus spoke of it at least 23 times as the *"Kingdom of Heaven,"* thus reminding the Jews, that he had not come at this time to set up an **earthly kingdom**.

Proof # 3

Many of the prophecies found, only in Matthew, were fulfilled, when Jerusalem was destroyed in 70 AD, and thus, were written particularly to the Jews.

If we understand this fact, as we approach the Matthew portions, we will see a beautiful harmony.

Matthew was written to the **Jews,**
Mark to the **Romans,**
Luke to the Greeks.

I. Matthew Exceptions:

Matthew 5:27-28

*"Ye have heard that it was said by them of old time,
Thou shalt not commit adultery:* ***but I say unto you,*** *(here's
that* **pivotal point of final authority)** *that* ***whosoever
looketh on a woman*** *to lust after her, hath* ***committed
adultery*** *with her already* ***in his heart."***

Permit me to insert one pertinent question here, for **those
who teach that adultery is grounds for divorce** today. **If so,**
how would they **apply** this teaching? Would a wife, request that
a divorce be granted, because she **saw a gleam in her husband's
eye, when he looked at another woman?**

**Jesus did not teach adultery or moral uncleanness as a
grounds for divorce,** but rather, as **an opportunity to manifest
Christ-like forgiveness.** Many married men today, are living
with their wives, with **hearts full of adultery,** while going to
church regularly. The only difference between them, and
exposed adulterers, is that **up until now,** they have kept it inside.
In God's sight, they're **still adulterers,** and need to repent.

Matthew 5:31-32

*"****It hath*** *been said,* ***whosoever shall put away*** *(divorce)
his wife, let him give her a writing of divorcement:* ***but I say
unto you,*** *(pivotal point of final authority) that whosoever
shall put away his wife, saving for the cause of* ***fornication,***
*causeth her to commit adultery: and whosoever shall marry
her that is divorced committeth adultery."*

97

Matthew 19:3-7 states:

*"The Pharisees also came unto him, **tempting him**, and saying unto him, Is it lawful for a man to put away* (divorce) *his wife for every cause?* (Do you agree with Hillel, the liberal?) *And He answered and said unto them, Have ye not read, that he which made them at the beginning made them male and female, And said, For this cause shall a man leave father and mother, and shall cleave to his wife: and they twain shall be one flesh? Wherefore they are no more twain, but one flesh. What therefore God hath joined together, let not man put asunder. They say unto Him, Why did Moses then command to give a writing of divorcement, and to put her away?"*

Notice here, that when Jesus told them what he believed, they grasped it, and immediately said, "That's different from what Moses told us. How do you justify contradicting Moses?" The Pharisees **knew** that Jesus was teaching **a different message** from Moses, about marriage and divorce. They as much as said, "Well, if you say **that**, and you're such an authority, then **why did Moses** teach something else?   **Are you** contradicting **Shammai, Hillel, and Moses**?"

We need to examine Deuteronomy 24:1-4, and bring its teaching into perspective, to see why it cannot apply to today.

Deuteronomy 24:1-4

*"When a man hath taken a wife, and married her, and it come to pass that she **find no favor in his eyes**, because he hath found some **uncleanness** in her; then let him write her a bill of divorcement, and give it in her hand, and send her out of his house. And when she is departed out of his house, she may go and be another man's wife. And if the latter husband hate her, and write her a bill of Divorcement, and giveth it in her hand, and sendeth her out of his house; or if the latter husband die, which took her to be his wife;*

98

Her former husband, which sent her away, may not take her again to be his wife, after that she is defiled; for that is abomination before the Lord: and thou shalt not cause the land to sin, which the Lord thy God giveth thee for an inheritance. "

Using this portion, many pastors and teachers say, divorced people, who have married another spouse, could never return to their first partners, *"for that is abomination. "*

The application of this Old Testament principle to New Testament situations, is unscriptural, and unfounded, for three reasons.

This Mosaic law:

☞ Was **born out of disobedience** *"hard heartedness"*.

☞ God the Father, and Jesus Christ, disclaimed the Father's authorship to it.

In Jeremiah 3: verses 1, 8, and 12-14, God the Father, spoke to this Deuteronomy 24 portion.

Jeremiah 3:1

*"**They say**, If a man put away his wife, and she go from him, and become another man's, shall he return unto her again? shall not that land be greatly polluted? but thou has played the harlot with many lovers; yet return again to me, saith the Lord. "*

Please note that **God** did not say, "I said." Instead he said, *"**They say**."* He is quoting here Deuteronomy 24:1-4, and says, this is what *"they say."* See how he proceeds to refute that principle, by his own actions toward Israel and Judah. The Living Bible says, *"But though you have left me and married*

99

many lovers, yet I have invited you to come to me again, the Lord says."

Jeremiah 3:8

God says he put backsliding Israel away. *"And I saw, when for all the causes whereby backsliding Israel committed adultery, I had put her away and **given her a bill of divorce;"** (God divorced Israel.)

Jeremiah 3:12

*"...**return**, thou backsliding Israel, sayeth the Lord;"* After divorcing Israel for her adulteries, God said, "come back to me."

Jeremiah 3:13

God gives to Israel, his answer to their problem, and for their healing. *"Only **acknowledge thine Iniquity**, that thou hast transgressed against thy Lord God,"* He says, first of all, admit your sin for your healing to begin. Then in verse 14, the Lord goes on to conclude his answer for their healing.

Jeremiah 3:14

*"Turn, O backsliding children, sayeth the Lord, **for I am married unto you**:"* First God said, admit it. Then he said, repent (quit it). Why should they quit it? Because **Israel was still his wife**.

If God the Father, truly initiated Moses to write Deuteronomy 24:1-4, then why did he speak of it as, *"**They say**?"* Why then didn't he follow that pattern himself, in dealing with Israel?

God explains why he didn't follow the Deuteronomy 24 pattern in Malachi 2:16:

Malachi 2:16

*"For the Lord, the God of Israel, says **he hates divorce** and cruel men. Therefore, control you passions—**let there be no divorcing of your wives.** "* (Here is God's view of marriage.)

Jesus himself, concurred with what his father said in Jeremiah 3, when he told the Pharises, in **Mark 10:5**, *"for the hardness of your heart, (**Moses**) wrote you this precept."* Note: Jesus did not say, "my Father wrote you this precept," but **"Moses wrote you this precept."** *"because of the hardness of your heart. "*

☞ **Jesus** made that Mosaic principle of no more effect, when he said, in Matthew 5:32 *"but I say unto you. "*

Note Jesus' response to this Deuteronomy teaching, as found in **Matthew 5:31, 32**. In Verse 31, Jesus said, *"It hath been said,* (He is speaking of the Old Testament Principle, found in Deuteronomy 24), *Whosoever shall put away* (divorce) *his wife, let him give her a bill of divorcement. "* If this Old Testament Principle, found in Deuteronomy 24, were still in effect, Jesus missed a perfect chance to say so right here.

If this portion were still valid today, then proper hermeneutics (the science of biblical interpretation), would say that several other teachings in the book of Deuteronomy should also be in effect today. Let's note a few of those other teachings, from the book of Deuteronomy:

Deuteronomy	**15:12,13**	Slavery
	21:10-14	Treatment of women prisoners
	21:15	Multiple wives
	21:18-21	Stoning of rebellious children
	23:2	No bastards (10th Gen.)

Which, of the present day Bible teachers, who are teaching **Deuteronomy 24:1-4** as still valid for today, are also teaching that these other portions of Deuteronomy should still be in effect also? None! If not, why not? Why should **Deuteronomy 24:1-4** still be valid, and none of the above portions? It's because they know the other portions went with the old covenant, and ended with the new one. The practice of the Old Testament principle of **Deuteronomy 24**, although practiced in Jesus' day, was disowned by God the Father, in Jeremiah 3, and ended, when Jesus stated, in **Matthew 5:32**, *"But I say unto you,"* and **Matthew 19:8,9** when Jesus said unto them, *"Moses, because of the hardness of your hearts, suffered you to put away your wives:* (Old Testament Principle). *But from the beginning* (God's original command) *it was not so. And I say unto you* (New Testament Principle) *whosoever shall put away his wife, except it be for fornication, and shall marry another, committeth adultery: and whoso marrieth her which is put away doth commit adultery."*

To completely understand how radically, clearly, and concisely, Jesus ended the Mosaic teaching, we only have to look at his **disciples shocked response**. When they heard him say these words, they knew that Jesus had just **ignored** Shammai and Hillel (the two rabbinical schools of thought in Jesus' day); and then had **closed the door** on the old Mosaic Principle completely, when he said unto them, *"But I say unto you."* In other words, that program is finished, concluded, over! Realizing this, and looking for some solution to the new information that they had just received, the disciples espoused an unrealistic conclusion, in Matthew 19:10.

Matthew 19:10

*"His disciples say unto him, If the case of the man be so with his wife, **it is not good to marry**."*

What did Jesus tell them, that made them say that? Did he just agree with Hillel, or Shammai, or Moses? If he had, the disciples probably would have said, "We already know that." But instead, they as much as said, "You've got to be kidding, Lord. Do you mean, we're **stuck for life**? Do you mean **you've closed down** Moses' law of marriage and divorce? If that's so, it's better **never to get married**!"

These disciples knew what Jesus had just said was completely new, concise, and contrary to what they had ever known before. They knew the old Mosaic way was gone.

Note what other commentators have to say about the Mosaic divorce principle.

Barnes on New Testament:

"Matthew 5:31,32 'Our Savior brought marriage back to its original intention...This is now the law of God. This was the original institution...Nor has any man or set of men - any legislature or any court, civil or ecclesiastical - a right to interfere, and declare that divorces may be granted for any other cause...No earthy laws can trample down the laws of God, or make that right which he has solemnly pronounced wrong.'"

In **Matthew 19:10**, when Jesus said, *"and I say unto you,"* the emphasis should be placed on the word "I". This statement, declared the opinion of Jesus Christ, as he had received it, directly from His Father. This he now proclaimed to be the law of his kingdom. This was a clear command of God, superseding the present day rabbinical teachers, and the teachings of Moses, from that time and ever after.

Indulgence had been given by the law of Moses, but that indulgence was to cease, and the marriage relationship, was brought back to God's original intention.

Weiss' Commentary of Matthew:

"Matthew 5:31,32 'In Jesus' eyes marriage is indissoluble. Accordingly, he who dismisses his wife and thereby gives her the liberty to marry another man, causes her to commit adultery, since her first marriage is still valid in the eyes of God...Whoever marries a woman who has been dismissed, himself commits adultery, since in God's eyes she is still the wife of her former husband.'"[9]

To see the clear contrast between the Deuteronomy 24 teaching, and Christ' New Testament teaching, we only need to look at Mark 10:6-8. Moses said a couple could separate, but Jesus said in Mark 10:6-8:

Mark 10:6-8

"*But from the beginning of the creation God made them male and female. For this cause shall a man leave his father and mother and* **cleave** (Greek: *kollaomai* - be glued, joined inseparably) *to his wife. And they* **twain** (Greek: *duo* - two) *shall be* **one flesh***: so then they are* **no more twain** (two) *but* **one** (Greek: *mia*) *flesh.*"

The phrase "**no more**" in the Greek is *Ouketi*

ou - not

keti - longer

---

[9] By Bernhard Weiss, <u>A Commentary on The New Testament, Vol. I, Matthew and Mark</u>, D. D., Copyright 1906, Harper Collins Publishers, N.Y.

To truly understand the permanency of what Jesus was saying, we must see how this same word is used, in other verses of the New Testament.

Mark 14:25
*"I will drink **no more** of the fruit of the vine."*

Did Jesus ever celebrate the Lord's supper with his disciples again while here on Earth? No! **No more** - not any longer - not any more - not again - denying absolutely. This is what the word, **no more,** in the Greek means.

John 6:66
*"Went back and walked **no more** with him."*

This means they never followed him again - not any longer - not again - **no more**.

Acts 8:39
*"And the eunuch saw him (Phillip) **no more**."*

That means no longer - not any more, ever - not again. Therefore, based upon these verses, when Jesus said, *"**They are no more twain**,"* (duo - two) it means, they are never again, no longer, not any more, two; but one flesh. **How long are they one flesh?**

Paul said, through direct revelation from Jesus Christ, the following:

Roman 7:2
*"For the woman which hath an husband is bound by the law to her husband **so long as he liveth**,"* (no more twain - never again until death).

I Corinthians 7:39

*"The wife is bound by the law **as long as her husband liveth**; but if her husband be dead, she is at liberty to be married to another."* (One flesh for life.)

Jesus said again in Luke 16:18

"Whosoever putteth away (divorces) *his wife, and marrieth another, committeth adultery; and whosoever marrieth her that is put away from her husband, committeth adultery."* This is the clear and concise New Testament Principle, that Jesus established, thereby cancelling the Old Testament Principle of Deuteronomy 24. It was cancelled when he said, *"they are no more twain but one flesh for life."*

Again Jesus said in Mark 10:9-12:

Mark 10:9-12

*"What therefore God hath **joined** together* (Greek: *suzeugnuo - to yoke together*), *let not man put **asunder*** (Greek: Chorizo - put apart) *and in the house his disciples asked him again of the same matter and he saith unto them, whosoever shall **put away*** (Greek: *apoluo - to loose away. Vine: to divorce*) *his wife, and marry another, **committeth adultery against her**. And if a woman shall **put away*** (divorce) *her husband, and be married to another, she committeth adultery."*

The only way this could be true, is to know that Jesus said, the partners of the first marriage, **can never again be twain (two), until death.** Because of the **universal marriage covenant**, established by God, in the Garden of Eden, **any** man and woman (saved or unsaved), who, each coming for the first time to pledge themselves to each other, are, by stating their intentions of commitment before God, **permanently glued** together, **by divine**

authority. ("*What therefore God has joined together, let not man put asunder.*") Why? Because they can **never again** be twain, but one, until death, according to the New Testament Principle.

The concession, made by Moses, and later refuted by God in Jeremiah 3:1, 8 and 12-14, and by Jesus in Matthew 5:27-32 and 19:3-12, has never been consistent with the scriptural teachings from Genesis 2:23-24, on up to when Jesus said, "*but from the beginning it was not so.*" The whole Bible teaches us that marriage is for life; that we must be willing to forgive our spouses who offend or hurt us, even as God, through Christ, has forgiven us.

Again I say, there are many today, who believe that adultery constitutes grounds for divorce. But, as you study the Old Testament, you will find that **adultery was never grounds for divorce**. Adulterers, under the Mosaic law, in Deuteronomy 22:22-24, were stoned to death. **Under the new covenant,** Jesus taught forgiveness and repentance. In John Chapter 8, Jesus forgave the woman, caught in the very act of adultery, when he said:

John 8:11
> "*Neither do I condemn thee: go, and sin no more.*"

In the **International Standard Bible Encyclopedia**, (Vol. II, pg. 865) Mr. C. Caverno in his article entitled "Divorce in the New Testament," says:

> "The scriptural doctrine of divorce in the New Testament is very simple. It is contained in Matthew 19:3-12.
> **We are not called upon to treat of divorce in the Mosaic legislation** *(sic)* (Deuteronomy 24:1-4). That was passed upon by Jesus in the above discussion and **by him ruled out of existence** in his system of religion. After Jesus had spoken as above, **the Mosaic permission of divorce**

107

became a dead letter. There could not be practice under it among his disciples. So such Old Testament divorce is now **a mere matter of antiquarian curiosity**...

But here as in numerous other instances, Christ went behind the enactments **to primitive original principles** whose recognition would make the law of none effect, because no practice was to be permitted under it. Thus **the Old Testament is disposed of**."[10]

Again let me remind you of the pivotal phrases which Jesus used over and over:

Matthew 5:27-28
*"you have heard it said: **But I say unto you.** "*

and again in

Matthew 19:8b-9
*"but from the beginning it was not so, **and I say unto you,** "*

Whenever Jesus said this phrase, he was actually saying, "forget what you thought was right before, for whatever reason. This is what My Father and I really meant. **This truth today, supersedes all present distorted teachings**."

Other examples of this are found in Matthew 5:21,22 and 27,28. The first teaching, was clarifying what constituted murder. Then he elaborated God's real meaning.

---

[10] International Standard Bible Encyclopedia: Copyright 1939 Wm. B. Eerdmans Publishing Co., Grand Rapids, Michigan.

Matthew 5:22

"*But I say unto you* (there's that phrase again) *whosoever is angry with his brother without a cause shall be in danger of the judgement.*"

Jesus deepened the truth, by saying, you don't have to physically kill a person to be a murderer, but "*as a man thinketh in his heart, so is he.*"

John interprets this portion for us further in I John 3:15.

I John 3:15

"*Whosoever hateth his brother is a murderer;...*"

From the old testament meaning of the physical act, a new, deeper meaning, was put into effect, when Jesus said, "*but I say unto you.*" The concept of murder was no longer just a physical act. Instead, to hate a brother in your heart, is the same as murder, in God's sight. It is no longer just an outward act, but now also involves an inward attitude.

Again in Matthew 5:27,28 Jesus said,
"*Ye have heard that it was said by them of old time. Thou shalt not commit adultery.*" (Old Testament Principal)

Interpretation: Don't have physical sexual relations outside the marriage (or even think about it).

Jesus said in Verse 28, "*Whosoever looketh on a woman to lust after her hath committed adultery with her already in his heart.*"

By this, we know, that adultery is not a physical act, as much as an attitude of the heart, (New Testament principle). By these clarifications, Jesus was instituting a return to God's original plan.

When Jesus Christ came, God's Word says, He was "the **complete revelation of God.**" In John, Chapter 14, Jesus said:

John 14:9b
"If you've seen Me, you have seen the Father."

Again in Revelation Chapter 1 he said:

Revelation 1:8
"I am Alpha and Omega, the beginning and the ending saith the Lord,"

The full light of God's perfect will, was brought to the New Testament Church. God, through Jesus Christ, established His kingdom's rules, and sent the Holy Spirit to write it upon the fleshly tables of our hearts. The Lord said, that **from now on,** it's a **new dispensation**. Listen to Paul, to whom the Lord revealed the New Covenant, by divine revelation, while in the desert.

Acts 14:15-16
*"We...preach unto you that ye should **turn** from these vanities unto the living God...**who in times past*** (Old Testament times) ***suffered*** (Greek word "eaw" which means 'permitted', allowed it to **fall**, or **slide**).

Paul was saying, that **up to now,** God dealt differently with the nations. He permitted some things; He allowed some things to slide.

Do you know what a father means when he tells his son, "This time I'll let it slide"? He means, that for now **he'll overlook it**, but there's a time coming, when you'll know better, and then watch out!

I can remember my mother telling me as a boy, "Joe, I won't spank you this time, but you're storing it up." I knew what she meant. She was **letting it slide** for then, but walk lightly, for judgment was nigh. In Acts Chapter 14, Paul said to the men of Lystra:

> **Acts 14:15-16**
> *"God...suffered all nations to walk in their own ways."*

Again in Acts, Paul was speaking on Mar's Hill, to the Athenians, the **new covenant** message.

> **Acts 17:30**
> *"And the times of **this ignorance** (Old Testament times) **God winked at; but now..."***

When is **now**? It is since Jesus Christ has come, and the Holy Spirit has been given, to indwell every person, who through repentance and faith, chooses to follow him. **Now** the **full revelation** of God has come to us, through Jesus Christ.

> **Acts 17:30**
> *"...now **(God)** commandeth..."*

Not **asketh**, not **suggesteth**, but:

> **Acts 17:30**
> *"God commandeth all men."*

Is that universal?

> *"All men everywhere."*

It's there, as clear as daylight. **What** does God command *"all men everywhere"* to do today?

111

> *"...God...commandeth all men every where to repent:"*

What does **repent** mean? The Amplified Version of Acts Chapter 17 is even stronger.

Acts 17:30 (Amplified Bible)
"Such [former] ages of ignorance God, it is true, ignored and allowed to pass unnoticed; but now he charges all people everywhere to repent.—[that is], to change their minds for the better and heartily to amend their ways, with abhorrence for their past sins. "

This word *"repent, "* is one of the **most used**, but **least understood words** in the Christian's vocabulary today.   Its misunderstanding, is why so many men are still living by an Old Testament teaching, conceived by Moses, out of **necessity and concession**, for a people, unwilling to obey God's eternal laws. In Matthew Chapter 19, Jesus spoke to the Jewish leaders about a new standard. We will study this key word, in detail, later on in this book.

Matthew 19:8, 9a
*"He saith unto them, Moses, **because** of the hardness of your hearts **suffered you** to put away* (divorce) *your wives, **but** (**pivotal point**) from the beginning it was not so. And I say **unto you**, whosoever shall put away his wife, **except it be for fornication**, and shall marry another, **committeth adultery. "***

Notice the **great similarity** between these verses and the ones in Mark and Luke. To see just how much they are alike, let's experiment, by **rewriting** these verses. Let's **remove the "exception clauses,"** to see if they agree with the others, upon

112

which we have built our **scriptural premise** so far. **The same verses,** with just **the exception phrase removed**, look like this:

Matthew 5:32

*"But I say unto you, that whosoever shall put away his wife..., causeth her to **commit adultery**: and whosoever shall **marry her** that is divorced **committeth adultery.** "*

Matthew 19:9

*"And I say unto you, Whosoever shall put away his wife..., and shall marry another, **committeth adultery**: and whoso **marrieth** her which is put away **doth commit adultery.** "*

Isn't that amazing!   No contradictions!   The only problem, is deciding what the phrase, *"except it be for fornication, "* really means.   We can get some real insight, by testing the current translations and interpretations of this phrase. Let's attempt to fit these **so-called "enlightened interpretations"** of these Scripture portions, with **our premise verses,** to see if they will **agree**.

A. False Modern Interpretations

For example, the Greek word *"porneia, "* is translated in
1.   **Matthew 5:32**
    a.   *"fornication "* in the King James Version
    b.   *"unchastity"* in the New American Standard Bible
2.   **Matthew 19:9**
    a.   *"fornication "* in the King James Version
    b.   *"unchastity"* in the New American Standard Bible

The New American Standard Bible's translation of the word fornication, is implying that **any person** is **married**,

113

until, he or she finds, his or her partner, has been involved in **any form of unchastity** or **immorality**. **At that point,** that person, has the **right, not only to divorce,** but **also to marry another person**. The **assumption** logically follows, that **God has approved of the divorce,** and will therefore, **approve of their marrying another individual.**

Some have taught this perspective, from these verses in Matthew, using **Deuteronomy 24:1-4** as a proof text. They teach that if a husband or wife **does not fulfill all the sexual desires and drives** of their marriage partner, this constitutes **"reverse fornication"** and is grounds **for divorce,** and justification **to marry another person.**

The inappropriate scriptural basis, used to justify **this** distorted teaching of reverse fornication, is **I Corinthians 7:3-4.**

I Corinthians 7:3-4

"Let the husband render unto the wife due benevolence: and likewise also the wife unto the husband. The wife hath not power of her own body, but the husband: and likewise also, the husband hath not power of his own body: but the wife."

Imagine the **fear and bondage** this teaching would bring to the wife of a harsh, inconsiderate husband. She would be tormented with the fear, of not fulfilling any warped desire he might have, and thus feel **totally responsible** for the resulting divorce.

Some even teach that **impotency** (lacking in sexual power), is grounds for divorce, and justification to marry again. **It's a pity** that **Abraham** didn't know that. He could have gotten rid of Sarah, and started building a mighty nation years sooner. Had **Zacharias** known this teaching, we might never have had a John the Baptist, by Elizabeth.

These poor, unenlightened saints of God, never heard of **"reverse fornication."**

If one considers this view of impotency as being grounds for divorce, **it is frightening**. If this view were true, the only way a young girl today could avoid the possibility of being dropped by her future husband, would be for her to **"try out" her "potency"** ahead of time. Not **just** her capacity to physically perform, but **also her ability to bear children**, lest when she gets married, she finds out too late that she is impotent and infertile. Based upon this false teaching, if her husband discovered her physical limitations, he could summarily get rid of her, and marry another. One only need exercise their imagination, to see the **devastating effects** this doctrine could have on the Church, or on society; yet it's being taught today in some **so-called** evangelical, holiness, and charismatic circles.

Let's analyze the **modern interpretation,** that says that the phrases, *"except it be for fornication,"* means, that if my partner becomes involved in **any moral impurity, I have scriptural grounds to divorce and marry another**. I would not **have to**, but the phrase *"except it be for fornication"* gives me the **right**.

First, let me repeat, that **there is no Scripture** that says **adultery** is grounds for divorce. **I challenge anyone** to show me **one verse** that teaches it. In the Old Testament, an adulterer was stoned to death. In the New Testament, Jesus forgave the woman caught in *"the very act of adultery."* But notice his **basis for forgiveness,** *"go and sin no more,"* (i.e., **quit it)!** Jesus has **never** condoned sin; he promises to forgive sin, **only if we quit it**. Remember, Jesus has **never** saved a man **in his sins**, only **from his sins**. I John 1:5-7, tells us that **without genuine repentance, no sin** will be cleansed.

What is the true scriptural meaning of the word *"fornication?"*

B. An Examination of the Word "Porneia"—Fornication

1. **Definitions** of adultery and fornication, are very distinct:
   a. **Fornication—(Porneia in Greek)**
      (1) Illicit sexual relations between unmarrieds.
      (2) Premarital coitus. (Exodus 22:16, Deuteronomy 22:28-29, Matthew 5:33 and 19:9, John 8:41)
   b. **Adultery—(Moikeia,** and derivations thereof, **in Greek)**
      (1) The willful violation of the marriage contract and covenant, by either partner, by engaging in intercourse, or desiring to be with a third party.
      (2) Extra-marital intercourse. (Deuteronomy 22:22, Exodus 20:14, Leviticus 20:10, Proverbs 6:32-33, Matthew 15:18-20)

In Biblical use, it should be noted, that the term *"porneia,"* has a **broad**, a **narrow**, and **a definitive** usage. You will find that most scholars will agree to these uses.

2. **Broad use of Porneia**
In its **broad** use, *"porneia"* comes from a root word, which meant "to sell." Basically, this was used in reference to the selling of slaves for the purpose of prostitution. It includes adultery, perverted sex, bestiality, and whoredoms. This **broad** use, is found many times in the New Testament, and **is touted** by those trying to prove that fornication means **immorality of any kind,** as the **only use** found in Scriptures. This, of course, **is not the case**.

3. Narrow use of Porneia

In its **narrow** usage, we find "porneia," speaking specifically of **premarital, sexual intercourse.** We again will take the **clear verses,** to shed light on the **unclear.** In I Corinthians Chapter 7, Paul is speaking to **single people** specifically.

I Corinthians 7:1-2

"...*It is good for a man not to touch a woman. Nevertheless, to avoid **fornication,*** (illicit sexual intercourse; premarital coitus) *let every man have **his own wife,** and let every woman have **her own husband.***"

To try to apply the **broad use** of *"porneia"* (immortality of any kind), to this verse, is **totally unrealistic** and hermeneutically unsound. This is especially true, when one realizes that **Paul was speaking to Christians.**

Another example is in John Chapter 8, Jesus was telling the Jews that although they claimed to be sons of Abraham, their actions proved they were sons of Satan. In a demeaning response, the Pharisees said to Jesus in verse 41, referring to his own birth:

John 8:41

"...*We be not born of **fornication;**...*"

The Living Bible has it:
"*We were not born out of wedlock.*"

It would be an injustice to say that "**porneia**" in this usage meant whoredoms, adultery, perverted sex, or bestiality. The Pharisees were saying in today's language, "We were conceived by Abraham, and Sarah—not through Hagar or another. Spiritually, we are truly Hebrew." Their choice of words, however, bore a secondary meaning or implication of, "we're not illegitimately born, but you are."

4. Difinitive Use of Porneia

Another way "porneia " is used in the **narrow** way, is what we will call, the **definitive** usage. This means, an instance where, one uses specific terms, in contrast to general terms, to describe a situation. An example of this would be, "There is a basket of fruit." That is a narrow usage. If I said, "There is a basket of apples, pears, oranges, bananas, grapes, peaches, and nectarines," that would be the **definitive** usage. An apple is a fruit; an orange is a fruit, but an apple is not an orange, and an orange is not an apple. But each **is a fruit!** In I Corinthians Chapter 6, we again find a **narrow** usage of the word "porneia," being very **definitive**.

> **I Corinthians 6:9-10**
> *"...Be not deceived neither **fornicators**, nor idolaters, nor **adulterers**, nor effeminate, nor abusers of themselves with mankind, nor thieves, nor covetous, nor drunkards, nor revilers, nor extortioners, shall inherit the kingdom of God."*

All these conditions, described by Paul in these verses, could have been categorized as **immorality**, or **sin**, or **uncleanness**. But instead, Paul used **definitive terms**. In this instance, one could say, "Fornication is sin; adultery is sin, but fornication and adultery are not the same. Fornication (porneia), means **illicit sexual intercourse between unmarried people,** while adultery, (moikeia) means **extramarital sexual intercourse.**"

This is, therefore, **definitive,** narrow, and thus a clear example of the **singular usage**. Other examples can be found in Matthew 15:19; Mark 7:21; and Galatians 5:19-21.

When Matthew wrote, he wrote basically to the Jews, to prove Jesus Christ was the Messiah. He addressed himself specifically, to Jewish-oriented problems and questions, such as Messiahship, prophecy, misinterpretation of Jewish laws, engagement, marriage, and divorce.

When we approach the **"exception clauses,"** in Matthew Chapters 5 and 19, it is essential that we **keep this in mind,** for the sake of **proper interpretation**.

So far, we've shown that trying to make **fornication** mean **adultery, immorality**, or **unchastity,** violates the obvious truth of our **clear premise verses,** (Luke 16:18; Mark 10:11-12; I Corinthians 7:10-11, 39; Romans 7:2-3). If it meant **any** of those three things, then we must totally **eliminate** all the **clear, singular verses,** that we have studied so far, for they couldn't possibly be interpreted that way.

If **fornication,** in Matthew Chapters 5 and 19, does mean that **adultery, unchastity**, or **general immorality** are grounds for divorce, and the right to marry again while your first spouse is still living, then Jesus and Paul were **both in error**. If we believe they were in error in this important subject, how can we trust them on any other?

Jesus said, couples become *"one flesh."* Jesus also said that that *"one flesh"* relationship, **cannot be divided**. **Paul said,** in I Corinthians Chapter 7 (paraphrase): **If you separate**, stay single or remarry your only husband. If you divorce and marry another person before your first spouse dies, you are an adulterer or an adulteress; and unless you repent of this sin, you **shall not inherit the kingdom of God**.

Once we compare the **clear** Scripture portions with the **unclear** Scripture portions, the obvious begins to appear. To understand the **"exception clauses,"** we must understand what Matthew was **truly saying** to the Jews, in Matthew Chapters 5 and 19. We must understand the social idiosyncrasies, that had to be spoken to, by Matthew. When Matthew inserted the phrase *"except it be for fornication, "* he did so because of his Jewish audience, and their unique social customs, regarding an engagement. Many writers today, when reading the clear premise verses in Mark and Luke say: "You cannot take those verses alone; you must include Matthew, Chapters 5 and 19 along with them, for balance." My reply is, "Why should we enjoy a privilege the earliest believers never had?" What these men fail to realize is that **Matthew was written after Mark and Luke**. This **so-called exception, was not available at all,** when Mark and Luke were written. **The real truth** is, that it **is not an exception at all**. Once we understand the **historical significance** and **social relevance** of the "fornication exceptions," it is clear that Jesus, in Matthew Chapters 5 and 19 was being **totally consistent** with every other portion of Scripture, on the subject of marriage and divorce. He was **still** confirming the **universality** and **permanency** of the marriage law. He was **still** emphasizing his desire for our lives to be pure and chaste. But he was also showing the Jews, that the **concession** which Moses had written, was **ended**.

It was not necessary to speak to those idiosyncrasies in the Gospels of Mark and Luke. Remember, Mark was written to **the Romans**, and Luke was written to **the Greeks**. We'll now approach these clauses with this in mind, to see if a true, consistent interpretation can be found.

5.   Porneia and the Bethrothal Relationship

Before the time of Christ's earthly ministry, the Jews had established a unique social practice, called "**betrothal**." "**Betrothal,**" is a lesser-used word in our society. It is basically synonymous with the English term **engagement**. This period **begins** when a couple agrees to give themselves to each other in marriage, and **ends** in the actual marriage. Today, the man usually gives the young lady an engagement ring. That act and announcement, "usually" means they are through looking around, and are now making plans for the final wedding vows.

There are, however, some **significant differences** between the Jewish betrothal of Jesus' day and the engagement of today. These differences are significant. In Jesus' day, the young man would not drive the girl out to some romantic spot, or take her to a fancy restaurant, to present her with a ring. Instead, he would gather some of his friends and take them with him to meet the girl. Then, before those friends, as witnesses, he would ask the girl to marry him.

This meeting was not a spur of the moment decision on the part of this couple. In most instances, they had never dated, as we know of dating. Instead, when they were born, their fathers agreed that it would be nice to have their children marry. Once this was decided, the wheels for such plans were set into motion. From childhood, little Jacob was told how nice it will be when he and Esther marry (ficticious names). Then the two fathers' families, will be even closer.

When Jacob finally reached the right age, both he and Esther were knowledgeable of the plans made for them. Thus, when Jacob and his friends come to find Esther (fictitious names), she already knows his purpose for coming.

After Jacob asks Esther to marry him, and she publicly says "yes," Jacob would give Esther, either a letter stating what transaction had taken place that day, or some coins to seal the agreement. An example of the importance of this transaction, is given by Jesus, in Luke Chapter 15, concerning the lost coin.

Luke 15:8-9

*"Either what woman having ten pieces of silver, if she lose one piece, doth not light a candle, and sweep the house, and seek diligently till she find it. And when she hath found it, she calleth her friends and her neighbors together, saying 'Rejoice with me; for I have found **the piece** which I had lost.'"*

Doesn't that sound rather ridiculous? Why would she, having lost a quarter, spend five dollars for a party, when she found it? Have you ever been in the midst of a situation where a girl looses her engagement ring? Pandemonium reigns until it is found. The whole house is in an uproar, and nothing is left unturned, until it's found.

The same is true with the woman in this parable. She had received from her Jacob, the "**nuptial coins**." Then, she had lost one of them. Those coins, were the evidence of their contract, and they were a love gift that was **very precious** to her.

Besides the nuptial coins, based upon Jacob's financial standing, a **"mohar"** or dowry would be given to Esther's parents. From that time on, Jacob and Esther were **"betrothed,"** or **engaged to be married**. Here is where any similarity ends in this relationship, as compared with a typical engagement, or the relationship between any Roman or Grecian couple. In other societies, such as ours, if the couple, after being engaged, changed their minds, they would just break up and start over again. If the young man is fortunate today, he may even get the engagement ring back.

In the Jewish society, however, Jacob and Esther when "betrothed," their relationship was basically expected to consummate in marriage. Both of the parties, were working toward that time of final vows, with great expectancy. By that, I mean he quit looking, she quit looking, and others were not to try to break into that relationship. Usually within a year to eighteen months, they knew the wedding would take place, and then they would become *"one flesh"* in **God's sight**.

If Jacob and Esther ever decided to separate, they couldn't just call it quits. **A betrothed couple in the Jewish society had to get a legal divorce. Only engaged? Yes!** But **to separate**, they had to go through **a legal divorce. To understand what Jesus was saying, in Matthew Chapters 5 and 19, it is imperative that you see this!**

In Genesis 19, is a story of Lot in Sodom and Gomorrah. The two angels came, to warn him to leave, before God's judgement fell. When the Sodomites came to Lot's house demanding that Lot release the two angels to them, Lot said:

Genesis 19:8

*"Behold now, I have two daughters **which have not known man; let me, I pray you, bring them out to you."***

Genesis 19:14

*"And Lot went out, and spake unto **his sons-in-law, which married his daughters**..."*

Question: If the daughters were married to Lot's sons-in-laws, why hadn't they known a man? It says they were married, but knew no man. How is that possible? The Living Bible clarifies it for us.

Genesis 19:14

*"So Lot rushed out to tell **his daughters' fiances**."*

Although they were not married, but only **"betrothed"**, the King James version said, they were *"married"*. This practice was still being practiced in Jesus' day.

Look at Matthew Chapter 1. This is one of the most familiar stories in the Bible. I'm sure most people have either read it many times, or heard it read, yet **miss** a powerful truth that reveals this Jewish social idiosyncrasy. Read it very carefully!

Matthew 1:18-20

*"Now the birth of Jesus Christ was on this wise: When as his mother Mary was **espoused** (literally engaged) to Joseph, before they came together, she was found with child of the Holy Ghost. Then Joseph **her husband,** (just espoused, yet called her husband) being a just man, and not willing to make her a public example, was minded to **put her away privily**."* (Literally, he was minded to loose her, or **divorce her**. Though not married yet, Joseph was going to **divorce**

123

Mary.) *"But while he thought on these things, behold, the angel of the Lord appeared unto him in a dream saying, 'Joseph, thou son of David, fear not to take unto thee Mary, thy wife: for that which is conceived in her is of the Holy Ghost.'"*

Matthew 1:24-25

"Then Joseph being raised from sleep did as the angel of the Lord had bidden him, and took unto him his wife: and knew her not till she had brought forth her firstborn son: and he called his name Jesus."

Jesus, **being a Jew**, knew of this Jewish custom of betrothal, and the divorce requirement, to dissolve it. He had Matthew make provision for it in these portions of Scripture. This was not a **universal exception**, but rather, a **clarification** to the Jews, concerning the **betrothal relationship**.

Jesus was saying that if, during the time of engagement or betrothal, it be found that Jacob or Esther, or any other betrothed person, has committed **fornication**, (illicit sexual intercourse by **unmarrieds**) **then, and then only (before the actual marriage vows make you** *"one flesh"* **for life, in God's sight**), may you get divorced and marry another.

Once one understands the Jewish bethrothal relationship, these Scriptures come into **full agreement** with our **original—premise verses**, and there are **no contradictions**. This truth about the betrothal period, and legal divorce from the same, was not some obscure fact in Jewish life. Rather, it was a very important feature, acknowledged by every level of Jewish social life. When the wedding night came for a betrothed couple, the bride's home would be well lighted. In great anticipation, the bride's friends would watch along the path, between the bride and bridegroom's houses. Late at night, the torches could be seen coming down the path, as the bridegroom and his friends approached. Then the cry would come forth; "The bridegroom cometh! The bridegroom cometh!" In great excitement, the bride would come out to meet the bridegroom, and they'd return together, with their friends, to the bridegroom's home. On the way, neighbors would then come out and wish them well. At the bridegroom's home, would be a festive celebration, until almost midnight, when the traditional Jewish wedding would be performed, with the appropriate vows.

The final step in the Jewish marriage was for the bridegroom to take the bride into the *"bridegroom's chamber,"* and there to **enter into** the bride, and thus **tear the hymen**, giving evidence of her virginity.

This practice was **so important,** that the wedding of a virgin usually took place on a Wednesday, in order that if the husband wished to bring a charge that his wife was **not a virgin**, he might bring it immediately before the court on Thursday. The court met each Thursday morning to hear such things.

If evidence could be brought forth for such charges, there would be a public trial. One can read of such a trial in Deuteronomy 22:13-21. There, in verse 15, it talks about the *"tokens of a damsel's virginity,"* being brought forth by the bride's parents as evidence. This token was worn as a part of the bride's garment, at the time of the consummation of the marriage. The husband had to hand this token over **to the bride's parents** afterwards. It would bear traces of blood from the ruptured hymen, and was accepted as evidence of the bride's **virginity**.

In instances where the man was making a false claim against the bride, verse 19 says, he had to pay the father of the bride one hundred shekels of silver for the evil report he brought forth, and **was bound** to that bride **for life**. He couldn't take advantage of the concession, that Moses made for the hard-hearted Jews, by *"putting her away"* later.

If, however, it could be proven that the woman was not a virgin (had committed fornication before the actual marriage), the woman would be stoned to death, and the man would be free to marry again. **Deuteronomy 22:20-21.**

C. Comparing Scriptures

Let's take that phrase from this unclear portion, and compare it with **the clear,** to see if we can learn what it could be saying. Let's start by using Luke Chapter 16.

Luke 16:18

"Whosoever putteth away his wife and marrieth another, committeth adultery..."

Remember the visualization? Refer to Illustration #9.

Illustration #9

Legally married by society

Jesus called it adultery.

Based upon this verse, Jack **lusted for Sue**, divorced Jill, and married Sue. Jesus then said that Jack was committing **Adultery**! Adultery against **whom**? **Jill**.

The only reason it could possibly be adultery, is because **God supernaturally united Jack and Jill for life**. Refer to **Illustration #10**.

Illustration #10

Jack   Sue
Jesus calls this adultery

(Innocent partner in Divorce)

Sam   Jill
Jesus calls this adultery

If *"except it be for fornication"* means *"except it be for adultery,"* or means *"except for immorality or unchastity,"* then **Jill is now free to marry again**. **Right?** **This** is what is being preached today. **This is not** what **Jesus preached** however. We must decide **whose** teaching **we will** follow. Some say, **Jack** committed adultery **against Jill**, when he married Sue. Thus **Jill is free** now, since **that's**

127

moral uncleanness. True, it **is moral uncleanness**. It **is unchastity**. It **is adultery**. **But Jesus said Jill's** condition was still adulterous **even after Jack had married Sue**.

> **Luke 16:18**
> *"...and whosoever marrieth her* (Jill) *that is put away* (divorced by Jack) *from her husband **committeth adultery**."* Refer to **illustration #10.**

Jack divorced Jill, and committed adultery against Jill. Jack and Jill, were **still** *"one flesh"* **in God's sight**. **Jesus said it!**

If Jesus knew what He was saying in the **clear verses**, then those who interpret *"except it be for fornication"* to mean **adultery, immorality, or unchastity,** as related to a married person, are **wrong**. **It can't** mean any of these, and still concur with Christ's teaching.

II. The Pauline Exception:

We now come to **the so-called Pauline exception**. Before we examine it, let me say that so far, when one considers and understands the historical setting involved, **all of the Scriptures harmonize perfectly**. There are **no loose ends,** and **no contradictions**. The **"exceptions,"** which are **not exceptions**, but **clarifications,** given for a Jewish tradition, agree completely with the **clear** Scriptures discussed above. Thus, our **basic convictions** should become even stronger. This is again confirmed by the Apostle Paul in I Corinthians Chapter 7.

> **I Corinthians 7:10-16**
> *"And unto the married I command, yet not I, but the Lord, Let not the wife depart from her husband: But and if she depart, let her remain unmarried, or be reconciled to her husband: and let not the husband put away his wife. But to the rest speak I, not the Lord: If any brother hath a wife*

that believeth not, and she be pleased to dwell with him, let him not put her away (or divorce), *And the woman which hath an husband that believeth not, and if he be pleased to dwell with her, let her not leave him. For the unbelieving husband is sanctified by the wife, and the unbelieving wife is sanctified by the husband: else were your children unclean; but now are they holy. But if the unbelieving depart, let him depart. **A brother or sister is not under bondage in such cases:** but God hath called us to peace. For what knowest thou, O wife, whether thou shalt save thy husband? or how knowest thou, O man, whether thou shalt save thy wife.*"

The condition of which Paul speaks here, is one of **two possible situations.**

A. First, a saved man or woman, in direct disobedience to the will of God, marries an unsaved person, and becomes *"**unequally yoked.**"* We need to notice that Paul describes this union as **being yoked, or joined**—which says that even when couples marry in rebellion to God's will, they are still made *"one flesh"* **by their vows or commitment.**

B. Second, it could be describing a situation where an unsaved couple are married, (made *"one flesh"* supernaturally by the **universal marriage law)** but one of them subsequently acknowledges his/her sin, repents, trusts Christ's sacrifice for his/her sins, and declare Jesus Christ as his/her Lord.

In either situation, Paul says, **the Christian must never initiate, or promote a separation**. Instead, he or she (the Christian), must do all he or she can to make the marriage work. The clause in question, and promoted as **"The Pauline Exception,"** is found in I Corinthians 7:15.

I Corinthians 7:15

*"...A brother or sister is not **under bondage** in such cases."*

Some today, who teach the traditional protestant view, say that this verse is giving permission to the Christian spouse, to divorce his/her unsaved partner. They claim this permission, is based upon the unsaved partner's not allowing their Christian spouse to live with them. To arrive at this conclusion, one must totally ignore and deny the universal marriage law, and **the supernatural act of God,** making two *"one flesh."*

This teaching could not be farther from the truth for three reasons.

1. This portion is not sanctioning divorce or adulterous marriages, unless Paul was double-minded. Remember, he stated just before this, in verses 10 and 11, that if a spouse left his/her partner, he/she was *"to remain unmarried, or be reconciled to her husband,"* **(or his wife)**. Paul reaffirms this truth in I Corinthians 7:39.

I Corinthians 7:39

"The wife is bound by the law as long as her husband liveth."

To say that Paul was presenting **conflicting Biblical standards** in the middle of these two clear portions, is **unthinkable**. Try to imagine the foolishness of saying that a man (Paul), under the inspiration of the Holy Spirit, in one chapter, taught in the following manner:

a. **Scene One**: "If you are married and separated, remain unmarried, or be reconciled to your partner."

b. **Scene Two**: "If your unbelieving spouse won't let you live with him/her, you can leave him/her, find a new partner, and start over with a new spouse."

c. **Scene Three**: "Remember, whenever you become married, and are made *"one flesh,"* by God, you are *"one flesh"* for life. The only way your covenant can be broken, is if one partner dies. Only then can you consider marrying again. For as long as your spouse lives, you are bound by the law of the marriage."

Wouldn't you think this pattern of teaching would be rather strange; rather inconsistent; rather schizophrenic? In order to show you that Paul was none of these, let's examine the two phrases, **"depart,"** and **"under bondage,"** a little more closely, to see how they can all agree with the clear portions of Scripture, relating to this same subject.

In I Corinthians 7:10,11:
"And unto the married I command, yet not I, but the Lord, Let not the wife depart from her husband: But and if she depart, let her remain unmarried, or be reconciled to her husband: and let not the husband put away his wife."

2. The word *"depart"*, *"chorizo"*, in the Greek, according to **Young's Analytical Concordance to the**

Bible, simply means, "to put apart." To put apart, only authorizes a separation. It in no way condones a divorce, or the freedom to marry another spouse. Here is **the only instruction God's word has today** for a marriage separation.

I Corinthians 7:11
*"...But and if she depart, let her **remain unmarried**, or be **reconciled** to her husband."*

3. The words in I Corinthians 7:15, *"under bondage,"* are being spoken, in this particular portion, specifically to the Christian partner, and says, if it becomes unbearable, and your partner will not let you stay, you don't need to remain there, in a state of servility, or in a state of being stepped on, abused, or treated like a slave. You are then free, to *"depart."* Again, let me say it **does not infer** a **right to divorce, or to marry another spouse—only to** *"depart."* You are married for life, but you may have to live separately, until reconciliation can be realized. This is very clear, and agrees with all the clear passages we have studied.

Please remember this important principle, when interpreting any portion of the Scripture.

When the unclear portions are interpreted properly, they are in total agreement with all the clear Scripture portions.

God's Word, is very clear on this point, that God, supernaturally makes all couples *"one flesh"* **for life!** **There are no exceptions, or contradictions!** **We can no longer go back**

132

to the Old Testament provision of convenience for *"hard-hearted"* people.

It is also interesting to note another confirmation of this position, in I Corinthians Chapter 7.

I Corinthians 7:15

*"But if the unbelieving depart, let him depart. A brother or a sister is not **under bondage** in such cases: **but God hath called us to peace"***—to unity—to agreement—to reconciliation—not to divorce!

The word, *"peace"* in the Greek, is **eirene,** and means peace, unity, agreement. This speaks of **reconciliation,** and does not even suggest divorce and consecutive marriages.

III. Author's Note:

I know this truth seems **absolutely impossible** in today's society. Our churches are becoming filled with couples, in second, third and fourth relationships. These couples are not just at the layman level, but are now becoming prevalent among deacons, elders, pastors, Bible teachers and evangelists. Many of these same leaders, have **no intention** of changing their lifestyles. They will fight this truth till their death, lest they feel a need to repent. At the same time, many others have been deceived, and have innocently become participants, in promoting this humanistic philosophy.

Because this Erasmian View is so widespread in the Church, and churches are so infiltrated by couples in their second, third or sixth relationship, this message isn't popular. Nevertheless, heeding it is not only necessary, but mandatory, if the Lord Jesus is going to come for a church *"without wrinkle or spot."*

Ephesians 5:27

"...*not having spot, or wrinkle or any such thing; but that it should be holy and without blemish.*"

The Church, by ignoring this doctrine, or by offering in its place, a **cheap grace** (sometimes called "sloppy agape"), is permitting and promoting, consecutive polygamy, which is **totally contrary to New Testament truth**. Unless all of God's people (not just pastors) stand up and begin to declare, *"Thus saith the Lord,"* our society will fall, and the Church will have lost its *"saltiness."*

Section III

God's Requirement
and Provision

Chapter 7

Repentance

If the teachings thus far in this book are true and consistent with all Scripture, and the Church has been teaching error, then how should the present day Church respond?

☞   Should it continue as it has?

☞   Should it ignore these hard truths?

☞   Should it continue to promote consecutive polygamy, or accommodate it with rationalizations and men's misguided ideas? or

☞   Should it repent?

It must do, as Christ instructed the Church of Ephesus, in Revelation 2:5; *"Remember, repent and return."* To remember, **the church must go back to where it got off track.**

When did the present day Church begin to lose this truth, concerning marriage and divorce? **When did** corruption and compromise enter in? This happened **first, when the Church began to accept divorced and remarried couples into the Church, as a social norm**. **Secondly**, it happened when the Church replaced the message of repentance and commitment, with **unconditional forgiveness and easy believism.** Present-day believers cannot properly grasp the urgency of **restoring** this truth to the Church, without first understanding **the Bible doctrine of repentance**. May God **restore this truth** to His Church, so that true cleansing may come, before it's too late. In Acts Chapter 17, Paul, the apostle to the Gentiles, declared God's new program, for **bringing men into His kingdom**:

> **Acts 17:30-31**
> *"God...now commandeth all men every where **to repent**: Because he hath appointed a day, in the which he **will judge the world** in righteousness **by that man** whom he hath ordained;"*

Let's study the use of this word **repentance**, throughout the Bible. Observe the consistency with which repentance is stated, in Scripture, as being **a prerequisite and requirement, for true faith**. We will soon see, that repentance, was not only important in the Old and New Testament times, but **urgently** needs to be preached and practiced today.

I. Repentance in the Old Testament:

The Old Testament word for repentance, is *"shub."* The basic meaning of that word, is **having a radical change in one's view and/or direction**. In particular, repentance emphasizes the need for one to:

☞ **Radically change one's view of sin and of God**.

☞ No longer see sin, only in the physical sense, but to **see it, as God sees it**.

☞ Sinners and saints alike, are to have such an awareness of the holiness of God, that it causes not just sorrow: but **a conscious moral decision, to separate oneself from, and to forsake one's sin**.

Repentance, is illustrated by a picture of a man going away from God, and then turning around 180 degrees. **It is a quality decision,** to radically change one's spiritual direction, the outward evidence being, **a changed life**. **Repentance,** in the setting of *"shub,"* is **a complete turning away from past sins**. It does not mean sinlessness, but a changed attitude, direction, and purpose. It means that when one has stumbled and looks to get up, he is facing God, thus, progressing in the right direction.

The following verses carry out this thought, in describing one's attitude in approaching God.

A. II Chronicles 7:14

"If My people which are called by My name, shall **humble themselves...** *"*

This humbling, may take an outward form, but the outward form, is not the part that counts. It is **a decision**, and not **an emotion**; but may manifest itself outwardly, by emotion.

II Chronicles 7:14
"...shall humble themselves, and pray, and seek my face, and **turn from their wicked ways;"** *("shub"* turn)

If men will do this!
*"...**then** will I hear from heaven, and will forgive their sin, and will heal their land."*

Note:
- ☞ **It's not enough** to humble yourself and say, "I was wrong."
- ☞ **It's not enough** to pray, or even cry while praying.
- ☞ **It's not enough,** just to seek God's face.

God demands **repentance**. II Chronicles 7:14 goes on to say:
*"**Then, then** will I (God) hear from heaven and will forgive their sin, and heal their land."*

B. Proverbs 28:13

"*He that covereth his sins shall **not prosper**: but whoso confesseth and **forsaketh them*** (or leaves them) *shall have mercy.*"

We hear much about confessing Christ today, but little about **forsaking** past sin. **Without both, there is no promise of mercy**.

C. Isaiah 55:6-7

"*Seek ye the Lord while he may be found, call ye upon him while he is near: Let the wicked **forsake*** (leave) ***His way**, and the unrighteous man* (**forsake**-implied) *his thoughts: and let him **return*** (or turn again) *unto the Lord, and* (**then and only then**) *he will have mercy upon him; and to our God, for He will abundantly pardon.*"

D. Ezekiel 18:21-23

"*But if the wicked will **turn** from all his sins that **he hath committed**, and keep all My statutes, and do that which is lawful and right, he shall surely live, he shall not die. All his transgressions that he hath committed, they shall not be mentioned unto him: in his righteousness that he hath done he shall live. Have I any pleasure at all that the wicked should die? saith the Lord God: and not that he should **return from his ways**, and live?*"

E. Ezekiel 18:30b-32

"*...Repent, and **turn yourselves** from all your transgressions; so iniquity shall not be your ruin. **cast away** from you all your transgressions, whereby ye have transgressed; and make you a new heart and a* *new spirit: for why will ye die, O house of Israel? For I have **no pleasure** in the death of him that dieth, saith the Lord God: wherefore **turn yourselves,** (this* indicates **a quality decision** to alter your course) *and **live ye.** "*

These verses, plus many others, clearly indicate, that **repentance** was an **indispensable Old Testament prerequisite**, for fellowship with God.

II. Repentance in the New Testament:

In the New Testament, there are two words, "**metanoia**" and "**epistrepho,**" which are translated "**repentance**" and "**turn**" respectively.

A. Metanoia

"**Metanoia,**" means **to have another mind, or to change one's mind, opinion, or purpose**. In this case, it is to change one's mind, opinion, or purposes, **as it relates to sin**. To literally **see sin in a different light**—to see sin **as God sees sin**.

W. E. Vine in his <u>Expository Dictionary of Old and New Testament Words</u> says on page 281,

"In the New Testament the subject chiefly has reference to repentance from sin, and this change of mind involves both a turning from sin and a turning to God."[11]

---

[11]W. E. Vine, <u>Expository Dictionary of Old and New Testament Words</u>, Copyright© 1991, Flemming H. Revell, Company, New Jersey. Used by permission.

1. Peter Preached Repentance.

In Acts Chapter 2, Peter, was preaching his first post-Pentecost message, to open the door of the kingdom of God, to the Jews. It wasn't a message to just *"believe"* or *"confess."* When the Jews were pricked in their hearts by the convicting power of the Holy Spirit, they cried out to Peter and the other disciples, in verse 37b, saying, ***"What shall we do?"*** to be forgiven, cleansed, relieved? Peter's response was:

> ☞ **Change your mind, opinion**, and purpose about God, and your sins.
> ☞ **See your sin as God sees it**.
> ☞ **See your God,** as the holy, righteous, just and merciful God that He is.

Acts 2:38

*"...**Repent** and be baptized every one of you in the name of Jesus Christ for the remission* (or sending away) *of your sins, and ye shall receive the gift of the Holy Ghost."*

To reverse this phrase, one would have to say, "If you **don't repent** of your sins, in the name of Jesus Christ, your sins **won't be sent away**, nor shall you receive the gift of the Holy Ghost." That is **just as accurate,** and totally consistent, with basic New Testament concepts.

2. John the Baptist Preached Repentance.

In Matthew Chapter 3, John the Baptist declared:

Matthew 3:2

"...repent ye: for the kingdom of heaven is at hand."

3. Jesus Preached Repentance.

Here we have a **pre-pentecost** message, where **the indispensable prerequisite** for fellowship with God, is again "**repentance**." In Matthew Chapters 3 and 4, we see the baptism and temptation of the Lord Jesus. In Matthew Chapter 4, we hear our Lord's **first message,** to launch His ministry. It wasn't **rejoice**, or **believe**, or just **receive**, but rather:

Matthew 4:17

"repent, for the kingdom of God is at hand."

Again, in Matthew Chapter 9, Jesus was asked why he didn't fellowship just with those in his own denomination. Didn't he know, that God was only **in the Temple**? Why was he out among the riff-raf of society? When Jesus heard the Pharisees ask this of his disciples, he again clarified his calling and purpose. In Matthew Chapter 9, Jesus said:

Matthew 9:13b

"...I am not come to call the righteous, but sinners to repentance."

In Luke Chapter 15, Jesus was describing heaven's response, when men obeyed the New Testament message.

Luke 15:7

*"I say unto you, that likewise joy shall be in heaven over one sinner that **repenteth**..."*

4. The Disciples Preached Repentance.

In Mark, Chapter 6, Jesus sent out his twelve disciples, for their first evangelistic experience. He gave them power and authority, to confirm their message, with signs and wonders. Do you know **the only message** Jesus told his disciples to preach? It was the same message of repentance, as his had been!

Mark 6:12

*"And they went out and preached **that men should repent**."*

It's interesting to note, that when Luke writes of this same experience, he said, in Luke, Chapter 9:

Luke 9:2

*"...he sent them to preach **the kingdom of God**."*

Thus, **repentance,** is **the kingdom's message**.

In Acts, Chapter 3, Peter and John, went to the Temple, after the upper room experience. At the gate of the Temple, Peter was used of the Lord to bring healing to a man, crippled from birth. When the Jews saw it, they were amazed, and came en masse, to ask Peter and John what had happened. Peter then preached his second sermon. He said (paraphrased) "Don't come all unravelled over this. **We** didn't do it. If you remember, just a few days ago you crucified

Jesus, who was the Prince of Life. Well, God raised up the One you killed, and gave him authority, so that we could do this miracle, **in His name**. Jesus Christ, only **did** what the prophets said he would do, and, he **was** who the prophets said he was. You did in ignorance to him, the same things your ancestors did to the prophets. But, there is a way of forgiveness." That way of forgiveness, was to **repent**.

Acts 3:19
"Repent ye therefore, and be converted, that your sins may be blotted out..."

Acts 3:26
*"Unto you first God, having raised up his Son Jesus, sent him to bless you, in **turning away every one of you from His iniquities**."*

Let me also rephrase these verses? "If you **don't** **repent**, you **won't** be **converted**, and your sins **won't** be **blotted out**."

There is no verse, that states Jesus Christ will save you **in your sins**; only **from your sins**. **There is no other way**. Again in Acts, Chapter 17, we repeat Paul's message, to the Athenians.

Acts 17:30
*"And the times of this ignorance God winked at; but now **commandeth all men every where to repent**:"*

The Amplified Bible says:
*"Such [former] ages of ignorance God, it is true, ignored and allowed to pass unnoticed; but **now he charges all people everywhere to re-***

145

pent—[that is], to change their minds for the better and heartily to amend their ways *with abhorrence for their past sins."*

Again in Acts, Chapter 20, Paul called the elders of the church of Ephesus, to meet him in Miletus. There, he had a pastor's conference, where he reminded these pastors, of how their work was founded in Ephesus.

Acts 20:20-21

"And how I kept back nothing that was profitable unto you, but have showed you, and have taught you publicly, and from house to house, Testifying both to the Jews, and also to the Greeks,"

Here was the message Paul preached, and practiced, to establish the church of Ephesus. If the message was good enough for Paul, and for Ephesus, we should be preaching it. What was it?

First:
"Repentance toward God,"

and then secondly:
"And faith toward our Lord Jesus Christ."

Here is a post-Pentecost message of grace, that was preached by both Peter and Paul. A message that Paul said, was a complete message, to be preached by faithful and fearless men of God. The book of Ephesians, is evidence, that if we're willing to boldly proclaim it today, there will not be just *"fruit,"* but *"much fruit"*, and *"much fruit that will remain."*

B. Epistrepho

The next word found in the New Testament for "repentance" (or turn), is an even **more powerful word.** It is the word "**epistrepho.**" <u>**The International Standard Bible Encyclopedia**</u> says:

> "**The word is used to express the spiritual transition from sin to God...To strengthen the idea of faith...and to complete and emphasize the change required by N.T. repentance.**"[12]

1. Epistrepho, therefore, describes **the complete act and result of genuine repentance,** and is translated in the King James, by the word *"turn"* or *"turned."* Wherever it is used, it describes what has taken place, when **true repentance** has occurred, or **what should take place,** if and when true repentance does happen.

Epistrepho, implies a turning around. It is the changing of a sinner's mind and attitude, toward sin and God. It is only valid, when and where:

☞ **The intellect** is operating.

☞ **The emotions** are motivated.

☞ **The will** is active.

It goes far beyond grief or sorrow, to the point, where one comprehends personal sin as intolerable, before God's absolute holiness. This comprehension, results in the person:

☞ **Abhorring,** or hating his past sins.

☞ **Turning** one hundred eighty degrees from them.

☞ **Abandoning** them completely.

---

[12]<u>International Standard Bible Encyclopedia</u>, Wm. B. Eerdmans Publishing Company, Copyright © 1979, Used by permission.

2. The corresponding action to this renunciation of sin, is the person's receiving Christ's death in his behalf, and declaring Jesus Christ as his Lord and Master. This is **the total implication,** of the word **Epistrepho.**

The King James Version, translates it with a very quiet word, in contrast to its powerful implications. So quiet and mild is it, that it almost loses all impact on the reader.

To use the word *"turn,"* for this powerful truth, is like telling someone, that if they sit on a 100-megaton hydrogen bomb, and detonate it, it will tend to damage them some. It is a pity, such a word, was translated into the English language, with such an insufficient emphasis on its full implications.

a. In Acts, Chapter 9, you will see what I mean. Peter came to Lydda, and brought healing to Aeneas, who had been bedfast for eight years, with palsy. This really shook up the people.

Acts 9:35

"And all that dwelt at Lydda and Saron saw him, (Aeneas—living proof of the power of God) *and* ***turned to the Lord.***"

This portion should read: (Paraphrase) All that saw him, were stunned, and convicted that God was alive. They realized, as never before, that they were sinners, worthy of eternal punishment. They suddenly:

☞ **Saw** the awfulness of their sin.

☞ **Began** abhorring their past.

☞ **Making** confession to God, seeking complete forgiveness.

☞ **Committing** their lives to the Lordship of Jesus Christ.

This is what it is saying, by using the word "**epistrepho.**" The people en masse, heard, received, turned, and were born into the Family of God. What happened at Lydda, **must** happen in every person's life, if they are to be saved.

b. In Acts, Chapter 11, believers, who up to that time had been preaching only to the Jews, came to Antioch, and preached to the Greeks for the first time. Verse 21, quietly whispers to us the **explosive** result.

Acts 11:21
*"And the hand of the Lord was with them: and a **great number believed**, and **turned unto the Lord**."*

Actually, **there was a Holy Ghost revival,** that took place in Antioch. We even read later on in Acts, Chapter 11 that:

Acts 11:26b
"the disciples were called Christians first in Antioch."

That town was **turned upside down,** with men being changed by the dynamite Gospel of Jesus Christ.

Again, **"repentance"** is a New Testament message; and until an individual **repents, abhors, and forsakes his past sins, he just isn't saved**. That's what the Word says. To say a person has repented, without an evident change, is a pretense.

3. Dreading the thought of going to hell, in itself, is not repentance; but may cause one to come to true repentance. It's evidenced, by a changed mind, that causes a sinner to walk a new path, away from past sin.

a. **The intellect** must be involved, to accept truth, as to your condition. You believe what God has to say about your sins and concur with His abhorrence of them.

b. **The emotions** must come into play in response to truth. You begin to hate what you once loved—your sins. And you now love what you once hated—God.

c. **Your will** must act. You sense the need, count the cost, and act upon it.

☞ I **will** repent.

☞ I **will** turn to God.

☞ I **will** cast away my old sins, and turn in faith to Christ, for cleansing.

☞ I **will** make Jesus Christ Lord of my life from this day forth.

4. In saying this, I am not preaching salvation by works anymore than Paul was, when he said in Acts, Chapter 20:

Acts 20:21
*"Testifying...**repentance** toward God, and **faith** in our Lord Jesus Christ."*

Repentance is not salvation, but a condition or attitude, to which one must come, to receive genuine salvation. There is no meritorious value in it. In itself, one cannot earn salvation. It is psychologically impossible to place yourself before God, for the forgiveness of sin, and be loosed by God from those sins, unless you **sincerely renounce and turn your back** on everything that is at variance with God.

Just as the New Birth is impossible without **faith**; true, **saving faith** is impossible without **genuine repentance**. These go together like thunder and lightning. Thunder isn't lightning, and lightning isn't thunder. Yet, like repentance and faith, they are mutually involved. Where one is, you'll find the other, for neither is independent of the other. **We must get this truth down into our souls!** This is Bible truth! **Bible preaching is incomplete,** if the sinner is not brought face to face with repentance. Luke, Chapter 18, is an illustration of the necessity of a right attitude in approaching God.

Luke 18:9-14
"And He (Jesus) *spake this parable unto certain which **trusted in themselves** that they were **righteous**, and despised others. Two men went up into the temple to pray; the one a*

151

*Pharisee, and the other a Publican. The Pharisee stood and prayed thus **within himself,** God, I thank thee, that I am not as other men are, extortioners, unjust, adulterers, or even as this Publican. I fast twice in the week, I give tithes of all that I possess. And the Publican, standing afar off, would not lift up so much as his eyes unto heaven, but smote upon his breast, saying, God be merciful to me a sinner. I tell you, this man went down to his house justified rather than the other: for every one that exalteth himself shall be abased; and he that humbleth himself shall be exalted."*

Someone once said, **"Repentance** is the **negative** side of **faith,** and **faith** is the **positive** side of **repentance." One cannot separate the one from the other,** and have a **genuine Christian experience.**

This truth, is not being preached in many churches today. Thank God, however, there is still a remnant who do. The appeal we hear in some churches today says, **"just try Jesus,"** as though our Lord were like a pair of shoes to put on. The implication is, if the shoes (Jesus), feel good, we can keep them, but if they pinch, don't worry—something else might work later.

Again we hear, **"Only believe in Jesus, and you'll be saved."** If anyone cares to, they can check the error of that message in the Bible.

James 2:19-20

*"Thou believest that there is one God; thou doest well: **the devils also believe and tremble.** But wilt thou know, **o vain man,** that faith without works is dead?"*

The Living Bible is clearer yet.

"Are there still some among you who hold that 'only believing' is enough?... Well, remember that the demons believe this too—so strongly that they tremble in terror! Fool! When will you ever learn that believing is useless without doing what God wants you to? Faith that does not result in good deeds is not real faith."

James is saying again, that the **true Christian experience, involves much more than believing**. It should be such a revolutionizing experience, that you're highest goal will be to do God's perfect will. Church members today, will give many **non-scriptural** reasons for believing they are true Christians, and sincerely believe they are.

I remember a man I met one time, who told me he was "a born-again Christian." I had already heard that the man was a "practicing alcoholic." He practiced it regularly. One day I said to him, "Tell me of your experience, when you became a Christian." As he began to speak, his eyes lit up with excitement.

"I was driving my pickup truck home one night about six years ago, all by myself. All of a sudden, I saw this bright light all around me, in the cab of my pickup. It was the most peaceful thing I ever experienced! From that time on, I knew it was God, and I had been born again."

After further questioning, I found out that the man had been drinking heavily at the time. Nothing I could say about repentance or change, could shake his faith in "that experience." I even quoted I Corinthians, Chapter 6.

I Corinthians 6:9-10

"...Be not deceived...neither drunkards, nor...shall inherit the kingdom of God."

He trusted "his experience"—he **believed**! I believe I Corinthians 6:9-10, teaches that that man went to a drunkard's grave.

Some may say, "that's judgementalism." No, it's not. I'm saying what God's Word says. I'd rather say what God says any day, than just make people feel good about themselves. I've heard some say, "God hates divorce, and marriage is for life, **but** God is love, and where ever you are, you're fine." That, my friend, is **devastating compromise,** and shall be judged by God as such. I'll put my confidence in God's eternal word, because of what Jesus said about it, in Luke, Chapter 21.

Luke 21:33

*"Heaven and earth shall pass away, but **my** words shall not pass away."*

That man, **sincerely believed** in his experience, and consequently, **never repented** of the sin of drunkenness.

When Zacchaeus, the chief publican (tax collector), was forgiven, there was an immediate change of attitude and motive. Luke, Chapter 19, tells us:

Luke 19:8

"...Behold, Lord," (That's a good start. Someone has said, that if Jesus isn't **Lord of all**, He isn't Lord **at all**.) *"Behold, Lord, the half of my goods I give to the poor; and if I have taken*

any thing from any man by false accusation, I restore him fourfold."

Zacchaeus, did not do this **to be** saved, but **because he was saved.** His outlook on what was important in life, took on a totally new perspective. It was judged now, in the light of eternity. Note the next verse.

Luke 19:9
*"And Jesus said unto him, **this day is salvation come to this house.** "*

The Living Bible says it this way:
*"This **shows** that salvation is come to this home today."*

Today one hears, "I'm a Methodist," or "I'm a Baptist," or "I'm a Catholic," implying that these membership relationships, are synonymous with repentance and faith. I read recently, that "one's label" is useless, in the light of eternity. If one is truly in the River of Life, the label will wash off. If he's not, after death it will burn off. This illustrates, that **we do not enter heaven by labels,** no matter how fine that denomination may be. **Nowhere in God's Word,** do we find that Christ is coming for a Methodist, Baptist, Pentecostal, etc., but rather, for those who *"love his appearing."*

Even if I'm a pastor, an evangelist, a deacon, an elder, or if I have the gift of prophecy, experience visions, dance before the Lord, pray in my own prayer language, cast out demons. Even these manifestations are not proof that I am born again. Satan is a deceiver and a counterfeiter. He will be glad to keep you

155

occupied, or give you counterfeits of these same gifts to play with, if in doing so, he can make you **think** you don't **need** to repent. The Egyptian soothsayers, duplicated most of the miracles Moses performed before Pharaoh. Who gave them that power? It doesn't matter what my office may be—if I'm nine-gifted, one-gifted, or if I can shout and pray the bark off an oak tree; if I've never **repented of my past sins, I am lost,** according to God's Word.

Look at Matthew, Chapter 7, where Jesus is speaking.

Matthew 7:21-23

*"Not every one that **saith unto me,** Lord, Lord, shall enter into the kingdom of heaven; but he that **doeth the will of my Father** which is in heaven. many* (note this now—these people are convinced, active, religious people speaking) *many will say unto me in **that day**,* (What day? The great white throne judgment. They have already missed the Judgment seat of Christ, and are really surprised!) *Lord, Lord, have we not **prophesied in thy name?*** (They did everything in the name of the Lord Jesus Christ) *and in **thy name** have **cast out devils?*** (These people, even went further in Christian type ministries than the majority of ministers today; they confronted the supernatural world.) *and in **thy name** done **many wonderful works?*** (Please understand something here, Jesus didn't argue with their claims. Their lives evidently revolved around church work. But listen!) *And then* (when they finished their claims) *And then will I profess unto them, I never* (When?) *never knew you: depart from me, ye*

that work iniquity. (another translation says) *ye that work lawlessness. "*

These verses, remind me of the story of the man who came to bat for his team. There were two outs, and the score was tied, at the bottom of the ninth inning. He hit the ball deep into center field on the first pitch. On the way out to catch the fly ball, the center fielder slipped and fell. The batter was a very fast runner. Before the center fielder could get the ball back into home plate, the runner was in, for an in-park home run. The crowd went wild, and the team met the runner at home plate, with great jubilation. **He knew** that he had hit a home run. **The team knew** that he had hit a home run. **The crowd knew** that he had hit a home run. There was joyous pandemonium. But then, someone noticed the right foul-line umpire. He was signaling an unbelievable sign! All eyes were suddenly fixed on the umpire, in stunned silence. Then, the umpire's voice could be heard to say,

"**You're out!**"

"**Out**? Why that's impossible! Didn't you see the hit?"

"Yes."

"Didn't you see me run the bases?"

"Yes."

"Didn't you see me cross home plate long before the ball came in?"

"Yes."

"Then what do you mean, I'm out?"

Then the sad news came. "You are out, because, in your rush to get home, you failed to **touch first base**. Therefore, **you're out!**"

I believe Jesus was saying the same thing. He said, (paraphrased) "Yes, I heard your prophecies;

157

yes, I saw your exorcism; yes, I saw all your works; **but, you missed first base. You never repented of your past sins.** Oh, you confessed them, but you never repented of them, and thus, *I never knew you.*"

"**You're out!**"

Luke 13:3

"except ye repent, ye shall all likewise perish."

A.W. Tozer once said,

"**A converted man is both reformed and regenerated. Unless the sinner is willing to reform his way of living, he will never know the inward experience of regeneration.**

The idea that God will pardon a rebel who has not given up his rebellion is contrary both to Scriptures and to common sense.

I think there is little doubt that the teaching of salvation without repentance has lowered the moral standing of the church and has produced a multitude of deceived religious professors who erroneously believe themselves to be saved, when in fact they are still in the gall of bitterness and the bond of iniquity."[13]

The Scriptures are very careful to warn us of **areas**, where many will be deceived into thinking they are going to heaven, when in reality, they are not. Areas, in which the Word has made it plain, that God **demands total repentance before** we can enter the

---

[13] A. W. Tozer from "The Root of the Righteous", copyrighted by Christian Publications, Inc. Used by permission.

kingdom of God.   Paul, writing to the Church of
Corinth, gave this warning in I Corinthians Chapter 6.

I Corinthians 6:9-10

*"Know ye not that the unrighteous **shall not
inherit the kingdom of God?** Be not deceived*
(Living Bible: *'Don't fool yourselves'*) *neither
fornicators,* (Those unmarrieds who are still
practicing illicit sex, and have not had a change
of mind and direction in this area, to cause them
to turn 180 degrees in hatred, abhorrence, and a
willingness to forsake it.) *nor idolaters,* (Those
who are still worshipping another person, place
or thing, or are putting more value on any
person, place or thing, than on their relationship
to God; or praying to; worshipping or putting
their dependence for eternal life on anything or
anyone other than the Lord Jesus Christ; and
have not repented, or turned around 180 degrees,
away from it, with hatred, and abhorrence, to
forsake it.) *nor adulterers,* (Those once married,
who practice lusting after others in their minds.
Those who have put away their wives, and
married again, or married one that was put away,
and did not, or have not, had a change of mind,
and direction, to have turned 180 degrees from it,
with hatred, abhorrence, and a determination to
forsake it in repentance.) *nor effeminate,* (Those
men or women, who still practice **sodomy** and **all
of its ramifications**, and have not had a complete
change, and renewing of the mind, through
repentance.) *nor abusers of themselves with
mankind,* (Persons, who still are practicing
perverted forms of sex acts, with man or beast,
and have not changed their minds and directions

180 degrees, to abhor and forsake such acts completely.) *nor thieves,* (Those, who still practice thievery, larceny, robbery, in whatever form, and have not had a change of mind and direction toward it 180 degrees, to hate, abhor and forsake it completely.) *nor covetous,* (Those, whose practice in life is based upon greed, selfishness and possessiveness, with no indication of a changed mind and direction, to see this as sin, and thus to hate, abhor and totally forsake it. Such a person, doesn't have the first idea of Christ's ownership, or divine stewardship in their life.) *nor drunkards,* (Persons, who still practice a life of alcoholic debilitation, and have never had a change of mind, or changed direction, to hate, abhor and forsake that practice.) *nor revilers,* (Persons, who still practice a life of slandering other persons, and who try to foment strife and turmoil as a daily part of their lives, and have not evidenced a change of mind, and a turn around of 180 degrees: to hate, abhor and forsake this sin.) *nor extortioners,* (Persons, who still practice every form of deceitfulness, for the purpose of gaining, at the expense of another, and who have not experienced a change of mind in this area, that has caused them to turn 180 degrees, and hate, abhor and forsake that sin. **None of these:)** *"shall inherit the kingdom of God."*

Paul says, *"Don't be deceived;"* and Jesus said in Matthew Chapter 7:

Matthew 7:14

"...Strait is the gate, and narrow is the way...and few there be that find it."

We live in an age of Christian balloons, Christian yo-yos, Christian "born-again" political candidates, presidents, etc., until the term has been diluted, to cover almost anything anyone wishes it to cover. The true church, needs to redefine the **true boundaries** of the **kingdom of God,** by these Scripture verses.

You and I have a choice—either **believe what Paul said,** under the inspiration of the Holy Spirit, **or what we see.** We must remember, that *"man looketh on the outward appearance, but God looketh on the heart."* (I Samuel 16:76) People can be very religious, enthusiastic, charismatic, know all the right words and phrases that saints are supposed to use, and **still be lost, if they have never repented of these conditions**.

In saying this, let me again emphasize that **I am not speaking of sinlessness, or earning our salvation**. I am speaking of one's **"quality decision,"** concerning these sins. A person may still stumble and fall in these areas, through ignorance of the devil's devices, or immaturity of Christian character. In either instance, that person, if a genuine Christian, will respond to that fall or weakness, with sorrow, confession, and repentance. With David of old, he will cry:

Psalms 51:1-4

"Have mercy upon me, O God, according to thy loving kindness: according unto the multitude of Thy tender mercies blot out my transgressions. Wash me thoroughly from mine iniquity, and cleanse me from my sin. For I acknowledge my

transgressions; and my sin is ever before me.
Against Thee, Thee only, have I sinned, and done
this evil in Thy sight."

To continue in, and practice, any of the above
sins, with the attitude of, "Well, God knows my heart"
or "I'm a new creature in Christ, and am under grace"
is to **show one's ignorance** of a genuine Biblical **new
birth** attitude.   Paul   confirms   this   again   in   I
Corinthians, Chapter 6.

I Corinthians 6:9-11a
*"Know ye not that the unrighteous **shall not
inherit the kingdom of God**? Be not deceived:
neither fornicators, nor idolaters, nor adulterers,
nor effeminate, nor abusers of themselves with
mankind,   Nor   thieves,   nor   covetous,   nor
drunkards, nor revilers, nor extortioners, **shall
inherit the kingdom of God**.   And such were
some of you..."*

Paul said that these very people were now saints!
"How can that be so, if what I'm saying is right?" Paul
said that the Corinthian saints, were "**at one time**" all
of these things, and now were saved.   **Never let
anyone tell you these people cannot be saved.** Jesus
Christ came to save **these very persons**.

III. The Result of Repentance:

In Matthew, Chapter 9, Jesus said:

Matthew 9:13
*"...I am not come to call the righteous, but **sinners to
repentance**."*

162

The misunderstanding today, is **the process, by which they are saved**. The process, contrary to what some would tell you, is not, "**just believe**." Remember again, that this is made very clear, in James, Chapter 2:

James 2:19
"Thou believest that there is one God; Thou doest well:
The devils also believe and tremble."

You and I know, that a devil shall not inherit the kingdom of God, just because it *"believes."*

Those described, in I Corinthians 6:11, were saved **the Bible way**. Paul, **never implied,** that these people were **still practicing** the unrighteousness, of verses 9 and 10. See what he said, in verse 11.

I Corinthians 6:11
*"And such **were** (past tense) some of you; but ye **are** (present tense) **washed,** but ye are **sanctified,** but ye are **justified** in the name of the Lord Jesus, and by the Spirit of our God."*

Paul said, that you are saved, because you came in the name of Jesus, and allowed the Spirit of God, to accomplish a special work within you.

Let's analyze, what Paul said happened to these Corinthian believers. First he said:

A. *"But ye are washed" - Apolouo I Corinthians 6:11*

This word *"washed,"* in the Greek, is "**apolouo**." "apo" meaning "away from," and "**louo,**" meaning **to wash all of, not just a part.** It means to be completely cleansed.

163

The New English Bible says:
"But you have been through the purifying waters."

What are these purifying waters, by which, we are to be washed? In Ephesians, Chapter 5, Paul speaking to husbands, said:

Ephesians 5:25-26
*"Husbands, love your wives, even as Christ also loved the Church, and gave Himself for it; That he might sanctify and cleanse it with the **washing of the water, by the word**."*

Jesus, addressed this same subject, in the Gospel of John, Chapter 3:

John 3:5
*"...Verily, verily, I say unto thee, Except a man be born of **water**...he cannot enter into the kingdom of God."*

John 15:3
*"Now ye are **clean through the word** which I have spoken unto you."*

The Word of God has a cleansing effect. Someone once said, "The Word of God will keep you from sin, or, sin will keep you from the Word of God." If you and I are ever saved, it will only be **one way, by faith**! But **faith in what?** Some say, "Faith in Jesus Christ." Is it **initially faith** in Christ, or, **faith** in **what the Word says about Christ?**

If you **reject the Word**, you won't trust Christ.

☞ **It's the Word** that tells us we're sinners, and need a Savior. If we reject that, we can't be saved.

☞ **It's the Word** that tells us Jesus Christ is God's Son. If we reject that, we cannot be saved.

☞ **The Word** tells us:

▸ Jesus was born of a virgin.

▸ Jesus lived a sinless life.

▸ Jesus died for us on Calvary.

▸ Jesus rose from the dead.

▸ Jesus ascended on high.

▸ Jesus is seated at the right hand of God as Lord of Lords and King of Kings.

▸ Jesus said, in the Bible that **we will be saved, if** we'll:

▹ **repent** of our sins,

▹ **believe** he died for us,

▹ **receive** him into our hearts by faith,

▹ and **make** him our Lord and Master.

If we will **receive** the Word, we are told:

☞ **faith** will be given to us,

☞ Grace will be given, which is God providing to us, "the power to know and do God's will"[14]

☞ and **cleansing** will come.

Before we can put our faith in Christ, we must believe **what the Word** says **about Christ**. Therefore, my **faith** is **based** upon **what the word says—all the word—not just the part I like.** In Romans, Chapter 10, Paul says:

---

[14] Bill Gothard's **Institute in Basic Youth Conflicts** , 1972. Oak Brook, Illinois. Used by permission.

Romans 10:17

"...*faith **cometh** by hearing,* (it isn't already there, but comes), *and hearing by the word of God.* (Rhema—that which God quickens to my heart)."

Whenever one **receives the Word,** cleansing comes. John, in I John Chapter 5, tells us, that the signs of that cleansing, are evident.

I John 5:1-6

"*Whosoever believeth that Jesus is the Christ is born of God: and everyone that loveth Him that begat* (God the Father) *loveth Him also that is begotten of Him* (Jesus Christ).*By this we know that we love the children of God, when we love God, and **keep His commandments**. For **this is the love of God**, that we **keep His commandments:** and His commandments are not grievous. For whatsoever is born of God overcometh the world, and this is the victory that overcometh the world, even our faith. Who is he that overcometh the world, but he that believeth that Jesus is the Son of God? This is he that came by water and blood, even Jesus Christ; not by water only, but by water and blood. And it is the Spirit that beareth witness, because the Spirit is truth.*"

The water is the Word, by which we are washed. The Spirit, bears witness to our hearts, that the Word of God is true, and we trust in the shed blood of Jesus Christ, **as revealed** through the Word, for our cleansing.

John, then speaks of **three witnesses**, as we continue on in the same chapter.

I John 5:7-13

"*For there are **three that bear record in heaven**, the **Father**, the **Word**, and the **Holy Ghost**: and these three are **one**. And there are **three that bear witness in earth**, the **Spirit**, and the **water**, and the **blood**: and these three agree in **one**. If we receive the witness of men, the witness of God* (the Word of God) *is greater: for **this is the witness of God** which he hath testified of His Son. He that believeth on the Son of God hath the witness in himself; he that believeth not God hath made him a liar; because he **believeth not the record*** (the Word of God) *that God gave of His Son. And **this is the record**,* (this is the message in God's Word) *that God hath given to us eternal life, and this life is in His Son. He that **hath** the Son **hath** life; and he that hath not the Son of God hath not life. These things have I **written** unto you that believe on the name of the Son of God; that ye may know that ye **have** eternal life,* (faith in the Word, brings faith in Christ) *and that ye may believe on the name of the Son of God.*"

1. Heavenly Witnesses

John, tells us of **three witnesses in heaven**. In the Scriptures, we are told, what they witnessed to us.

a. The Father—In Matthew, Chapter 17, God the Father, witnessed on the Mount of Transfiguration, concerning Jesus Christ's witness, thus:

Matthew 17:5

"*This is my beloved Son, in whom I am well pleased; **hear ye him.**"*

167

The Father's witness was, that one must hear what Jesus **said**, to know God's will for man's redemption.

b. The Son—The Living Word—In John, Chapter 6, Jesus confirmed the authoritative witness of His Word:

John 6:63
"...*The **words** that I speak unto you, they are spirit, and they **are life**.*"

Jesus said, (Paraphrase) "Listen to what I say, for my words, once received and obeyed, bring spiritual life."

c. The Holy Spirit—In John, Chapter 14, Jesus spoke of the third witness.

John 14:26
"*But the Comforter, which is the Holy Ghost, whom the Father will send in My name, He shall teach you all things, and bring all things to your remembrance, **whatsoever I have said unto you**.*"

The Holy Spirit, will **confirm** the cleansing words of Jesus Christ, to us. Again in John, Chapter 16, Jesus said:

John 16:14
"*He shall glorify me: for he shall receive of mine, and shall shew it unto you.*"

2. Earthly Witnesses

John, then goes on to tell us of the **three witnesses on earth.**

I John 5:8

*"And there are three that bear witness in earth, **The Spirit, The Water,** and **The Blood:** and these three agree in one."*

a. The Spirit—The same Spirit, that witnesses in heaven, witnesses and confirms God's, and Christ's reality, on earth also.

b. The Water—The Word of God, declares God's message to fallen mankind. The Word we possess on earth is:

☞ *"Forever, O Lord, thy Word is settled in heaven"* (Psalms 119:89)

☞ *"The Words of the Lord are pure words: as silver tried in a furnace of earth, purified seven times"* (Psalms 12:6)

☞ *"For thou hast magnified Thy Word above all Thy Name."* (Psalms 138:2)

We can **only** declare a complete washing and cleansing experientially, when we allow the *"washing by the Word"* to do its complete work, by responding to it, through *"repentance and faith"* (Acts 20:21):

☞ **Repentance** toward our old ways,

☞ **Confession** of sins,

☞ **Receiving** forgiveness through Christ's provision on Calvary, and

☞ **Declaring** with our mouths, that from that moment on, **the risen Lord Jesus Christ, is and shall be our Lord and Master**.

If you and I have professed to be born-again Christians, and have not **turned** from our past sinful practices, **our faith is not a scriptural faith,** and thus, is **not a saving faith. A saving faith, is a cleansing faith.** In II Timothy, Chapter 2, Paul says:

II Timothy 2:19b
*"...The Lord knoweth them that are His. And let every one that nameth the name of Christ **depart*** (The Greek word **aphistemi**: to place off from. This suggests an active decision on our part.) ***from iniquity*** (from unrighteousness or wrong).*" We will deal with this more extensively in this chapter, when we study II Corinthians 5:17.

c. The Blood

When God, the Holy Spirit, convicts a person, He convicts them on a basis totally consistent **with all the Word of God**. Those individuals, being genuinely convicted by the Holy Ghost—Who says, one must repent of his sins, will begin to see themselves in a new light. They will begin to see themselves as lost and deserving hell. They will begin to **see sin, as God sees sin**. Desiring to be saved, those convicted sinners, will renounce and forsake their past sins. They will seek Christ's cleansing, as the truth of God's Word, becomes a real experience to them, through faith. Then **the blood** will be applied. By obeying God's Word, they experience a cleansing.

I John 1:7

"...The blood of Jesus Christ his Son cleanseth us from all sin."

Revelation 1:5

*"Unto him that loved us, and **washed us** from our sins in his own blood,"*

I Corinthians 6:11

*"...But ye are **washed**."*

B. *"But ye are sanctified" – Hagiázo*

This word sanctified in the Greek, is "**hagiázo**," which means to separate **from sin** unto God, **from that** which is profane, to a sacred use.

It should be noted that in the Old Testament, whenever something was **sanctified** for God's use, it was **thoroughly cleansed first,** and then sanctified, for sacred use. If you and I are sanctified, **a complete cleansing, through repentance and faith,** preceded it. Paul, gave the Scriptural order, in II Corinthians, Chapter 6.

II Corinthians 6:17-18

Step 1: *"Wherefore **come out from among them**, and **be ye separate**, saith the Lord,"*

Step 2: *"and **touch not** the unclean thing;"*

Step 3: *"And **I will** receive you, And will be a Father unto you, and ye shall be My sons and daughters, saith the Lord almighty."*

C. *"But ye are justified"* - Dikaióo

The Greek word here, is **"dikaióo."** Its simplest meaning is, "to declare not guilty." Paul, is saying in this verse, the following. If anyone is still practicing any of these listed lifestyles, and **gives no evidence of repentance or abhorrence toward them**, they're lost. It doesn't matter what they say. Their lifestyle, is the evidence that they've never been born from above. Don't be deceived on this point! If they're still living in any of these conditions, they are lost. Paul goes on to say, "You folks ought to know this, for you once were like that. But, you came to a point in your life, where you repented. This happened, because the Holy Spirit revealed to you the whole truth of God's Word, regarding sin. Once you were convinced of God's attitude toward those things, you repented." (not just grief, but a change of mind, that caused you to **turn** from those evil ways, and abhor your past sins, to the point of your abandonment of them). Then, in simple faith, you turned and trusted what the Word revealed about Jesus Christ's death in your behalf. You received by faith Christ's forgiveness and cleansing, and by an act of your will, you made Jesus Christ Lord of your life. Thus, you are no longer classified with those just described as lost. Instead, **by obeying God's Word, you are** *"new creatures."*

I Corinthians 6:11
> *"...washed...sanctified...but ye are justified in the name of the Lord Jesus, and by the Spirit of our God."*

This is why, in verse 11, Paul could declare, that they *"were such,"* but **no longer such. Never** let anyone say that you can achieve justification **by any other means,** because that idea is contrary to the Word of God.

IV. Confronting Present-Day Teachings:

The greatest defense mechanism, used by those teaching an "**easy believism**" message, is found in II Corinthians, Chapter 5.

II Corinthians 5:17
"Therefore if any man be in Christ, he is a new creature: old things are passed away: and behold, all things are become new."

Sympathetic teachers today, say it's like you're starting all over again. Even if you've been married and divorced many times before you made this decision, you are now a *"new creature, old things are passed away."* **You can forget the vows you made to God at your first marriage,** and are now free to marry another.

These teachers should understand, that **one cannot sympathize and minister at the same time, for sympathy is self-elevating, and therefore it is sin.** Just suppose, you are attending a Sunday morning service, in my church. I have just finished a very eloquent message (Naturally!). I give an invitation, for seekers to come forward to become Christians. In amazement, you watch as a large number of people come forward. To your surprise, you know many of these people, and are thrilled to see them respond. As I pray with each person or couple, I have them stand up for final counseling and presentation to the congregation.

A. The first ones, are **a young couple,** whom you know for a fact have been living with each other for five months, unmarried. As they rise, what would you think if you heard me say, "Now you are new creatures in Christ, *'old things are passed away, behold all things are become new.'* **You can now go on living in this unmarried state,** because **you are new creatures**, and God doesn't care about that, now that you are *"in Christ."*

If I told them **that**, you know it wouldn't agree with Scripture. **If they were truly saved**, they would recognize their relationship was illegitimate in God's sight, **agree** with God, and **refuse** to let it continue. They would **quit** the relationship, or **get married**.

B. What if two at the altar were **sodomites,** who you knew had lived together for six or eight years. Could I say, "You are new creatures in Christ. *"Old things have passed away. Behold all things are become new."* God now recognizes your relationship, as pure and undefiled, and sees you as *'one flesh.'* Go in peace."

You say, **"horrors, no!"**

I saw a Christian film, giving scriptural evidences, to prove that we are in the last days, before Christ should return. In that film, so-called **"Christian gays"** (**God calls them sodomites**), were interviewed. They told how they were born-again Christians and loved the Lord. At the same time, they were practicing sodomy, and promoting it in their own church. Their pastor was also a sodomite. I'm not stretching these examples. It's happening in churches across America today.

On the editorial page of **Christianity Today,** dated April 18, 1980, was an article entitled **"Homosexuality: Biblical Guidance Through a Moral Morass,"** it stated (Emphasis mine):

> "Many **Christians** who **are homosexual** feel that the burden of celibacy is too great for them to bear, and choose instead a permanent relationship with another **homosexual Christian**...To deny that they know Christ would be **to go beyond Scripture**...How should the church respond?...We can only pray that they—and all Christians, **heterosexual** and **homosexual** alike—will be willing with equal boldness

174

to **face up to the clear teaching of Scripture.**"[15]

If only Lot had known this, maybe he could have turned Sodom and Gomorrah into model Christian cities, since they didn't need to repent. **No!** The Bible says, in I Corinthians, Chapter 6:

I Corinthians 6:9-10

*"Know ye not that the unrighteous shall not inherit the kingdom of God? Be not deceived: **Neither**... the effeminate, nor abusers of themselves with mankind* (sodomites)...*shall inherit the kingdom of God."*

The Scripture, says very clearly, that the sodomite shall not inherit God's kingdom, **unless he repents.** If they've repented, they'll have had a change of mind and of direction, 180 degrees. They will now hate, abhor, and forsake their past sins. When they do, Jesus describes to us the end result, in John, Chapter 8:

John 8:36

"If the Son therefore shall make you free, ye shall be free indeed."

C. Suppose one of those who came to the altar, was a **known prostitute,** who had made her living with men, seven days a week. What could I tell her? Could I tell her, that she is now *"a new creature, old things are passed away and behold all things are become new?"* Could I tell her, that from this day on, she should pray before she goes out

---

[15] **Christianity Today,** "Homosexuality: Biblical Guidance Through A Moral Morass, April 18, 1980, Carol Stream, IL 60188. Used by permission

on the streets, and ask God for an opportunity to witness to her customers, and lead them to Christ in bed?

If you say, "That's ludicrous!" You're right. If she is truly saved through repentance and faith, she will leave her past sin, even though it was a flourishing means of income for her.

D. If another person at the altar, were **a well-known thief**, the same answer would be true. "Turn, abhor, hate, and forsake your past sins. Cast them from you, if you are professing to have been born again."

E. Up to now, I have been using most of my examples, from I Corinthians 6:9-10. Let's go one step further. **Jack and Sue** come to the altar. Remember them? (Jack married Jill, met Sue, divorced Jill, married Sue.) It's three years later now, and Jack and Sue now have two children. Jill, Jack's first wife, is sitting in the back row of the same church, praying that Jack will be saved. She, after the divorce, was led to a salvation experience, by a neighbor. Since then, she has prayed daily, that Jack would be saved; and **there he was, at the altar,** with Sue.

After praying with Jack and Sue, how should I counsel them? Did you feel the mental twinge inside when I asked you that? Did you feel yourself groping for a different answer? Are you suddenly sensing a need to **rationalize** this one? Do you find it hard to say that Jack and Sue are living in adultery? **They are adulterers**, according to the eternal Word of God. They must repent, (forsake their past sins) even as the other sinners did, in order to be saved. You ask why? Because that is what Jesus said?

Luke 16:18

> *"**Whosoever**, putteth away his wife and marrieth another, committeth adultery."*

176

Did Jesus mean they only committed adultery the first night, or week, or month, or year? When does adultery cease to be adultery? When the children are born? Remember what Paul said, in Romans, Chapter 7.

Romans 7:3

*"So then, if **while her husband liveth** she be married to another man, she shall be called an adulteress."* (To say **he** shall be called an adulterer, would also be correct,)

How long is a fornicator, a fornicator? A harlot, a harlot? A drunkard, a drunkard? A thief, a thief? **Until they quit it!** Isn't that true? The real reason we have difficulty admitting it's still adultery, and must be repented of, is because **this society has accepted divorce, and the practice of marrying again,** as a **common thing**—the **accepted norm.** **Until that changes**, especially in the church, this sin will never abate, but rather, continue to spread.

What do I say to Jack and Sue? According to God's Word, they will **never** be *"one flesh,"* as long as Jill is living. Knowing this, **who am I** to say, *"'You are new creatures in Christ, old things are passed away, behold all things are become new?'* God, has blotted out the past, and now, He will bless this union, and make you *'one flesh'?"* Can I say that? If I do, what would Jill think? More importantly, **what would God say**? To say **that,** would be calling the Lord Jesus a **liar**, and calling evil good. I would also be guilty of failing to *"warn the wicked,"* as Ezekiel said, in Chapter 33.

Ezekiel 33:8-9

*"When I say unto the wicked, O wicked man, thou shalt surely die; if thou dost not speak to warn the wicked from his way, that wicked man shall die in his iniquity; **but his blood will I require at thine hand.** Nevertheless, if thou **warn** the wicked of his way **to turn from it**; if he do not turn from his way, he shall die in his iniquity; **but thou hast delivered thy soul. "**

Jill would probably say, "Here I've been praying for three years that he would be saved, and return to me and the children. Now he supposedly gets saved, and he's no longer **my** husband, but Sue's. Our vows are no longer valid, but those he made with Sue, are now acknowledged."

Don't you believe it! Until he repents, (forsakes that relationship with Sue) Paul and Jesus say, **he is still an adulterer**!

Luke 16:18

"Whosoever putteth away (divorces) *his wife and marrieth another, **committeth adultery:"***

I Corinthians 6:9-10

*"Be not deceived...**Adulterers shall** (not) **inherit the kingdom of God. "***

The New Testament, consistently teaches that an adulterer, is an adulterer, **until, he or she repents**—hates, abhors, and **abandons** his or her past sins.

I had a man say to me one night, "If that's my choice, this woman or Christ, then I'll take her, and go to hell." (He and the woman were not married. She had been married several times, and they were living together at this time)

I had to reply, "Sir, **that is your option!"**

I know, new Christians cannot be expected to respond immediately to life's situations, as a mature Christian would, but a new Christian's attitude, **hates sin**. He may stumble, but he will seek forgiveness and deliverance, and go on.

I believe I can describe what I'm saying, by this true illustration. A denominational district officer, was once called to a church in his area of responsibility, to oversee a board meeting, that was called to bring charges of immorality against the pastor of that church. This officer, didn't have to be there very long, to realize that the evidence was overwhelming against the pastor. Finally, when the truth was obvious, the officer asked the pastor, "This immoral relationship, was it a one-time thing, or did it happen many times?"

The pastor, knowing his sin had been exposed, retorted almost sarcastically and with no sense of remorse, "What difference does it make?" The wise officer, knowing the nature of man, said, "It is the difference between a **weak man**, and a **hog**." It is a **sheep's nature,** to stay out of the mud and filth. It is a **hog's nature,** to seek out the mud, because it feels cool to him. If one has truly repented of his sins and committed his life to Christ, he may stumble or fall from time to time, **but his attitude is different**. He's miserable when he disobeys his Lord, and is anxious to be forgiven.

I can tell you that I have not been without sin, through the years. I can say, however, that over forty-five years ago, I made a quality decision, to repent of my sins, and make Jesus Christ Lord of my life. That decision, allowed me to receive **a new nature** from God, and that new nature **hates sin**. I still sin, but I'm miserable when I do it. I know, and would confess to you, that it's wrong. My new nature, will **never** allow me to make excuses or rationalize, that "God knows my heart."

I believe, when the true Church of Jesus Christ finally comes to grips with this truth, and couples begin to realize, that with God, **there is no second choice**, they'll think twice, before leaping into second marriages or separations. Be assured of this however, as long as the **church** continues to compromise in this area, the church as we have known it, will disintegrate, and our families will be destroyed. All of this tragedy is occurring, because men of God today, refuse to say, *"it is written."*

F. Its True Meaning—II Corinthians 5:17

Let's look at II Corinthians, 5:17, now and see what it is **really saying**. Paul, has just talked about heaven, the judgment seat of Christ, the fear of the Lord, and our responsibility to live for Christ.

On this verse, Lenski says:
"Wherefore, if anyone (is) in Christ, a new creation (is he). The old things have passed away, Lo, Things have become new!
Three short, incisive statements, and the third is exclamatory. There are no connectives. This makes a statement sharper in the Greek, for the Greeks love to join everything so that when he omits connectives, he feels a jolt."[16]

Rather than giving comfort to those who think themselves safe with their sins *"in Christ,"* it declares, **the signs of a genuine Christian**. It's saying, "If you want to find a **genuine Christian**, here are the clear indications to look for."

---

[16]Interpretations of I & II Corinthians, by R. C. H. Lenski, Copyright © 1937, Lutheran Book Concerns, Used by Permission of Augsburg Press.

1. *"Therefore if any man be in Christ, he is a new creature..."* That's the proof of the pudding. He will not be anything like he was. Instead, you'll see in him, the *"fruit of the Spirit;"* **If** he has **truly** been born again. If he's not a new person, he's not **in Christ**.

2. *"...Old things are passed away..."* The Greek word for "passed," is **"para,"** which actually means "to pass away, or to perish." If anyone is **in Christ**, he is a new person, because he has perished, died to all his old past. That's the **sure sign** to look for.

II Timothy 2:19 says:
"...Let every one that nameth the name of Christ depart from iniquity."

That word, *"depart,"* in the Greek, is in the aorist tense, (the approximate equivalent of past tense in English) and implies that when a quality decision has been made in the past—*"nameth the name of Christ,"* the expected result of that decision, is **a complete severance** from the past, and a new direction realized—*"depart from iniquity."* Webster's Dictionary says of depart, "action took place **in the past**, without implication of continuance or repetition." Does that sound like **repentance** to you?

3. *"Behold all things are become new."* The word, *"things"* in the Greek, is in the perfect tense, and is the subject of the implied phrase, *"things have become new."* These *"things,"* became new in the past, and are constantly to remain so. R. C. H. Lenski in his book **Interpretation of I and II Corinthians** says:

181

"A new creation means that *'the old things have passed away,'* have gone *para*, have been cast 'aside.' These are the' *old things*' of the flesh, in which we at one time lived, which at one time were our love and our delight, which at one time filled our whole being. Paul is a master in using the singular and plural: *'a new creation'*—now *'the old things.'* A new unit—the entire mass of *'old things discarded.'* What would *'a new creation'* have to do with these good-for-nothing old things of the old Life? The Greek uses the aorist: *'did pass away,'* our idiom the perfect: *'have passed away.'* The aorist denotes one decisive past act by which the grand severance was made and the new creation was wrought. That is, of course, conversion or regeneration. And *'passed away'* is correct despite the fact that some of the old things still cling to us in this life. They only cling to the new creation; they are now *'old things'* and not really any longer a part of us.

So wonderful is this that Paul exclaims because of it by using the opposite: *'Lo, things have become new!'* *'All* things' in the A.V. is an importation of Rev. 21:5. But the R.V. is also mistaken with its rendering: *'they are become new'* i.e., *'the old things.'* They could not possibly become new; they had to be cast entirely away; other things had to take their place, things that were newly created. The subject of *gegone* is not drawn from *paralthen*; *'have become new'* contains its own subject, one that is implied in *kaina:* *'things have become new.'* The perfect tense signifies: *'became new in the past constantly to remain so.'* In these new things we live unto Christ." [17]

---

[17] Reprinted from INTERPRETATION OF 1 AND 2 CORINTHIANS by R. C. H. Lenski, copyright© 1937 Lutheran Book Concern. Used by permission of Augsburg Fortress.

So Paul, actually was saying to the saints in Corinth, *"If"* (this indicates that it is conditional):

☞ **If** this was your experience,

☞ **If** there came a time when the Holy Spirit convinced you of your lost condition,

☞ **If** that work caused you to grieve over your past sins, until you changed your mind, and found yourself hating, abhorring, and desiring to renounce and forsake them,

☞ **If** you, by an act of your will, separated yourself from those past sins, turned by faith, and trusted and appropriated Christ's death in your behalf, for the cleansing of your sins,

☞ **If** you yielded all your life to the Lordship of Jesus Christ from that day—**only then are you a** *"new creature."*

If you haven't experienced this transaction between you and God, then you may be religious, but you're not, "...a *new creation..."*

V. Romans 8:6-8 Clarified–Hupotasso:

Another portion of Scripture, used by many teachers of Scripture, **to disprove** what has been taught in this book, is found in Romans, Chapter 8.

Romans 8:6-8

*"For to be carnally minded is death; but to be spiritually minded is life and peace. Because the carnal mind is **enmity** against God: **for it is not subject to the law of God**, neither indeed can be."*

Concerning this portion of Scripture, some theologians surmise, that "Paul is declaring that the **natural man** can't possibly obey God's laws. Consequently, if it's impossible for the natural man to obey them, God **can't possibly** hold him responsible for **not** keeping them. **Therefore,** they conclude, **God doesn't recognize unbeliever's first marriages, divorces, or subsequent marriages.**"

Doesn't that sound good? Our only problem, is that **that isn't what it says at all**. Let me elaborate on these verses a little more.

The Greek word for *"not subject"* is **"hupotasso"** which is a military term. It means **to set oneself in array under**. In the U.S. military, there are privates, corporals, sergeants, lieutenants, captains, colonels, and generals. Each is a different rank, each **set in array under** the next. If a private tries to tell a sergeant to do something, he had better know how to say "Please, Sir." But if a drill sergeant tells a private to do something, the private **doesn't have to do it**; however, he'd better, if he knows what's good for him. He, by joining the U.S. military, has **set himself in array under** the sergeant.

That sergeant may weigh 145 pounds, be five foot four inches tall, and have only an eighth grade education. The private may be six foot ten inches tall, weigh 290 pounds and have a Master's degree. Again, I say, he doesn't **have to** obey the sergeant, but he'd better if he knows what's good for him. He has **set himself in array under that sergeant**. Even if that private knows his way is better, and that he has more insight than the sergeant, the sergeant is still representing the authority of the

U.S. Army, and the sergeant will reprimand him if he disobeys any reasonable order.

Let's look at a few Scriptural examples of this term, *"subject"*.

Luke 2:51

"...He (Jesus)...*was subject unto them* (Mary and Joseph)*"*

Luke 10:17

"devils are subject unto us (the disciples) *through Thy name."*

Ephesians 5:24

"...Church is subject unto Christ..."

I Peter 2:18

"Servants, be subject to your Masters..."

Being *"not subject,"* does **not** mean, that one is **not answerable or responsible** for their actions. Neither does it mean one will avoid any consequences for his unwillingness to be subject. If Jesus had not been **subject** to his parents, they would have been obligated to correct him. If saints are not **subject** or obedient to Christ, as they know they are supposed to be, then they are in disobedience, and the law of sowing and reaping comes into effect.

What Paul was saying here, was that **the carnal mind**, by an action of its own will and rebellious nature, **refuses** to submit to authority, or to **set itself in array under** God's authority. **This does not mean it is not responsible for its decisions, and resultant disobedience**; but simply means, that's the way the carnal mind functions. **Thus, all unrepentant sinners, who refuse to set themselves in array under God's commands, will**

185

still be judged by those divine commands at the Great White Throne Judgment.

Note to Pastors

Having been a pastor myself for over 30 years, I know that controversial subjects add stress to an already difficult situation. We pastors tend to avoid additional stress as much as possible. This is why we pastors today will have to have our minds renewed in this area of truth, and throw out all of the false information we have received in our theological training and Christian reading, before we can even consider teaching this truth. We won't be willing to pay the price it will cost us, unless or until, the Holy Spirit shows us that this is truth; until we get it down into our soul like a fire; until we are willing to pay any price (and there will be one to pay). If you're called to preach the whole counsel of God, be obedient to your calling.

But please remember, if you preach the Word uncompromisingly, God will honor you!

The closest comparison I can find in the Scriptures to the reception of this message by many pastors, who know what preaching it would do to their churches, is where Jesus was confronted by the chief priests and elders in, Matthew, Chapter 21.

Matthew 21:23-27a

"And when he was come into the temple, the chief priests and the elders of the people came unto him as he was teaching, and said, By what authority doest thou these things? and who gave thee this authority? And Jesus

*answered and said unto them, I also will ask you one thing,
which if ye tell me, I in like wise will tell you by what
authority I do these things.   The Baptism of John, whence
was it?   from heaven or of men?"* **(Notice the response
here!)** *"and they reasoned with themselves, saying, If we
shall say, from heaven; he will say unto us, Why did ye not
then believe him?   But if we shall say, Of men; we fear the
people; for all hold John as a prophet.   And they answered
Jesus, and said, we cannot tell."*

The chief priests and elders, **never once,** considered how to
answer the question **truthfully!** They weren't even concerned,
whether or not the answer they would give would be right or
wrong.   **Their only concern, was, if they answered, what
would be the social repercussions from that answer?** Their
main worry was, if we say yes, then **this** will happen, if we say
no, then **this** will happen. We don't like the results **either** answer
will bring. Whether one is right or wrong is superfluous; it is a
no win situation either way we answer—so we just won't answer.

I've had pastors say, "I can see what you are saying is
scriptural, but I wouldn't **dare** preach it in **my church!** I can't
however, support divorce, family break down, or multiple
adulterous marriages anymore, because I've now received
additional light." I know their struggle is real, and difficult.

The end result of the Pharisees' dilemma, is like that of
many pastors today. They refuse to answer either way **for fear
of the possible results.**

Your greatest problem, as was mine, will be to take your
eyes off **what you see and hear today.** You will feel pressure
from those people who have been married, divorced, and are now
living in adulterous marriages, while vehemently and sincerely
believing that they are Christians. They, most likely, will be the
best workers, the best givers, and the most enthusiastic people
you have in your congregation, far outshining the majority of
your membership. Their enthusiastic religious conduct, however,

does not alter the clear teaching of God's Word. God's Word is *"like silver, seven times refined,"* and we are told to *"preach the Word,"* nothing else but the Word regardless of audience response. In John, Chapter 17, Jesus prayed:

John 17:17
*"Sanctify them through thy truth: **thy word is truth**."*

I Corinthians 6:9
*"The adulterers...**shall** (**not**) inherit the kingdom of God."*

Luke 16:18
*"**Whosoever** putteth away his wife, and marrieth another, committeth adultery."*

VI. Definition of Terms

Just believing doesn't do it; baptism doesn't do it; church membership or denominational affiliation doesn't do it. One only becomes a *"new creation in Christ,"* through genuine Biblical repentance and faith, with the accompanying evidence, being that Jesus Christ is Lord.

Some might ask, "Is this teaching **legalism**?"

No! What I have taught, is **New Testament Christianity**.

A. What is Legalism?
　　1. **Trying to earn your salvation, by good works.** I've never implied that.
　　2. **Trying to live the Christian life, in your own energy.** I have never implied that.

B. What is Condemnation?

Some may say, that this teaching constitutes a message of *"condemnation."* I appreciate the response that my son, Jeff, gave, when this charge was made, concerning his father's teaching of marriage and divorce. He said, "If that's how you receive my father's message, you must be receiving it in the context, of John, Chapter 3."

John 3:19-20
"And this is the condemnation, that light is come into the world, and men loved darkness rather than light, because their deeds were evil. For every one that doeth evil hateth the light, neither cometh to the light, lest his deeds should be reproved."

"I've listened to my dad's teachings on this subject, and have never felt condemnation. Maybe these verses explain why you are."

Several years ago, a professing Christian couple, came to my office very upset, upon hearing this message. After going over the Scriptures carefully, they each admitted to having been married several times, **before** making their decision for Christ." Finally, the man said, "Why can't God forgive us for our first marriage?"

I said, "Because your first marriage wasn't sin. Regardless of what the courts said, when they gave you the divorce papers, scripturally, you were only separated. It was your subsequent marriages, that constituted adultery. Whether you recited your vows one time, or a dozen times, doesn't really change the fact that you are still, *'one flesh,'* with the **first**, formerly unmarried person, with whom you made vows before God."

As they started to leave in frustration, still unwilling to accept this message, again he said, "I still don't see why God can't forgive our first marriage and divorce."

I replied, "What you're actually saying is, 'I refuse to repent, so why don't **You** repent, God, (change Your mind) about what is pure and holy?'" God's answer to that idea is found in Malachi, Chapter 3; Ecclesiastes, Chapter 5; Proverbs, Chapter 28; and Jeremiah, Chapter 7.

Malachi 3:6

" *...For I am the Lord, I change not...* "

Ecclesiastes 5:6 (The Living Bible)

"Don't try to defend yourself by telling the messenger from God that it was all a mistake (to make the vow). That would make God very angry..."

Proverbs 28:13

"He that covereth his sins shall not prosper: but whoso confesseth and forsaketh them shall have mercy."

Jeremiah 7:8-11 (The Living Bible)

"You think because the temple is here, you will never suffer? Don't fool yourselves! Do you really think that you can steal, murder, commit adultery, lie, and worship Baal and all of those new gods of yours, and then come here and stand before Me in my temple and chant, 'We are saved!'—only to go right back to all these evil things again? Is My temple but a den of robbers in your eyes? For I see all the evil going on in there."

If a person enjoys his/her present sinful state, **nothing** anyone can say or do will move him/her.

C. What is Grace?

A great problem today, is that many have misunderstood **the true nature of God's grace**. Grace, has come to mean, that **we can do as we please, when we please, if we please, where we please**; and God understands. Grace, has become **a license to sin,** rather than **a release from sin**. A good definition of what grace is not, and what grace is, follows:

1. **Grace is not:**

    a. **"God's indulgence of letting us do what we want."** Romans 6:1-2

    b. **"The removal of penalties for breaking God's law."** Galatians 6:7-8

    c. **"The replacement of God's law, but rather the desire and power to fulfill the principles behind the law."** Romans 3:31

2. **Grace is:**

    "An enabling force from God, giving all men the desire and power to do his will."[18]

Thus, the Covenant of Grace, **brings to an end** Old Testament interpretations of morality, and reestablishes a new morality, made possible and attainable, through the process of **repentance, faith, and commitment to Jesus Christ**.

D. Biblical Definition of Adultery

In Romans Chapter 7, Paul says, if someone divorces, and marries another, while their first partner lives:

---

[18] Bill Gothard's **Institute in Basic Youth Conflicts, 1972.** Oak Brook Illinois. Used by permission.

Romans 7:3

"she (they) *shall be **called an adulteress*** (or he shall be called an **adulterer**)*"*

What you and I might believe, is not the important issue here. The important question is; **What does The Word say?** I know people who don't believe in tithing, hell, healing, etc. That doesn't knock God off His throne, or change His Word! Regardless of their unbelief, the unchanging Word of God is still true. Their doubt and unbelief, does not affect its truthfulness or authority one iota.

One insight here, I believe the Scriptures teach **three aspects of adultery**.

First: is **the physical act of adultery**, such as was committed, and repented of, by David.

Second: is that **mental act of adultery** described by Jesus in Matthew, Chapter 5.

Matthew 5:28

*"But I say unto you, that whosoever **looketh on a woman** to lust after her **hath committed adultery** with her already in his heart."*

Third: is **the state of adultery.** It is of this condition that Paul speaks, in Romans, Chapter 7.

Roman 7:3

*"So then if, while her husband liveth, she be married to another man, she shall be called an **adulteress**."*

As long as a person remains in that condition, **regardless of his religious experience**, he is abiding in a **state,** or continuous **condition,** called **adultery.** A man in a prison uniform, being held against his will for some crime, and forbidden by the authorities to be set free, is **a prisoner**. He will continue to be called a prisoner or inmate, until the authorities release him, and his living conditions change. Even if you educate that man, give him lots of money, and put him in a nice wardrobe, he's still a prisoner. His condition, or state of being, is that of a prisoner.

Paul said that as long as one remains in the **position**, **condition**, or **continuous state** of being divorced and living with someone other than their first living husband or wife, they are to be called **adulterers/adulteresses.**

Romans 7:3
*"She shall be **called an adulteress.** "*

When will the church stop saying what the **world** says, and start saying what The **Word** says? The word of God's **universal marriage law** makes **two, one, "till death do us part."** May God help the Church to **repent!**

Oh, that God would send a revival like that today. To even suggest such a move of God today, brings labels of **legalism, bondage, or heresy,** from many church leaders. Regardless of their responses, I believe *"Jesus Christ is the same yesterday, today, and forever."*

Just as the Old Testament shows that there was a price to pay, to follow God, Jesus told us there is **a cost involved,** in following Him today.

Luke 14:26-27
*"If **any man** come to me, and **hate not** his father, and mother, and wife, and children, and brethren, and sisters, yea, and his own life also, **he cannot be my disciple. And whosoever doth not bear his cross**, and come after me, **cannot be my disciple.** "*

Verse 33

*"So likewise, **whosoever** he be of you that forsaketh not all that he hath, he **cannot be my disciple.**"*

He also warned us of the *"last days"* atmosphere. II Timothy, Chapter 3, in the Living Bible states:

II Timothy 3:1-5

*"You may as well know this too, Timothy, that **in the last days**, it is going to be **very difficult** to be a Christian. For people will love only themselves and their money; they will be proud and boastful, sneering at God, disobedient to their parents, **ungrateful to them** and thoroughly bad. They will be hardheaded and **never give in** to others; they will be constant liars and troublemakers and **will think nothing of immorality.** They will be rough and cruel, and sneer at those who try to be good. They will betray their friends; they will be hotheaded, puffed up with pride, and prefer good times to worshipping God. They will go to church, yes, but they won't really believe anything they hear. **Don't be taken in by people like that.**"*

II Timothy 4:3-4

*"For there is going to come a time when people **won't listen to truth**, but will go around **looking for teachers** who will tell them **just what they want to hear.** They won't listen to what the Bible says but will blithely follow their own misguided ideas."*

Our society, has accepted adultery, as a social norm. Thus, even the **compromising church,** caught up in and permeated by this disobedience, **rebels against the truth of God's Word.** They say, "that message just won't cut it in today's world; **this is a new age.**"

Jesus spoke about this in Mark, Chapter 7, in response to some Jewish leaders. When they criticized Him for going against their traditions. Jesus replied:

Mark 7:6-9 (The Living Bible)
"Jesus replied, You bunch of hypocrites! Isaiah the prophet described you very well when he said, 'These people **speak** *very prettily about the Lord but have no love for Him at all.* **Their worship is a farce,** *for they claim that God commands the people to obey their petty rules. How right Isaiah was! For you* **ignore** *God's* **specific orders and substitute your own traditions.** *You are simply* **rejecting God's laws and trampling** *them under your feet for the sake of tradition.'"*

Paul, warned Christians, to watch out for this very condition, creeping into the Church. Paul states, in Colossians, Chapter 2:

Colossians 2:8 (The Living Bible)
"Don't let others spoil your faith and joy with their philosophies, **their wrong and shallow answers built on men's thoughts and ideas, instead of on what Christ has said.** *"*

May the True Church of Jesus Christ **awaken, before it's too late.** It is time for Christ's body
- ☞ **To purge** itself of *"the leaven,"*
- ☞ **To repent** of it's compromising state,
- ☞ **To loudly proclaim** the message of **repentance, faith** and **obedience,** to a confused world and corrupted Church.

Chapter **8**

Forgiveness

Forgiveness, what a wonderful word! To forgive, according to the <u>World Book Encyclopedia</u>, is:

- ☞ "To give up the wish to punish or get even with."
- ☞ "Not to have hard feelings at or toward."
- ☞ "To excuse."
- ☞ "Remission of a debt, obligation, or penalty."

What a wonderful experience I had on June 13, 1951, kneeling at an altar, in a little white frame church, in Fremont, Nebraska. That was the night that I acknowledged all my sins to God, the Father. I told Him, that I desired to be set free from all my sins. I said, "I don't want any more of the addictive habits, bad attitude, anger, resentment, hatred, selfishness, or immortality in my life. Please forgive me, and wash them away in the precious blood of Jesus Christ. I believe, Jesus Christ died for all my sins, and shed his blood.to wash them away. I believe He did it for me, and by faith, I claim forgiveness for all my sins, in Jesus Name. Lord Jesus, I believe you are the Son of God, and by faith, I receive you into my heart as my Lord and Savior. Come in, and take complete charge of my life. I renounce all my old ways, and separate myself from them by an act of my will. I desire to love the things you love and hate the things you hate. Thank you for hearing my prayer, for receiving me, forgiving me, and indwelling me with Your Spirit. Thank you for making me your child."

When I rose from my knees, I knew something wonderful had taken place in my life; something beyond the natural realm. I found, that my desires and appetites, changed immediately. What I used to love, I now hated, and what I once hated, I now loved. I was a new creature in Christ. I was wonderfully **forgiven,** and set free from my past. My guilt, fear, alienations, and rebellion were gone forever! I experienced peace and joy, in a way I had never before known. That was 45 years ago, and that same joy and peace are still mine, because I know I am completely forgiven. It is still real today, because, when I first came seeking forgiveness, I realized receiving Jesus Christ, must be preceded by repentance, and a firmly fixed intention, not to repeat those sins again. I am not speaking of perfection, but **a new intention** and desire, to please God, because of a new nature that He placed in me, when He quickened my heart, to allow it to respond to His prompting. Thank God for the assurance found in I John 1:7.

I John 1:7

"...*the blood of Jesus Christ His Son cleanseth us from all sin.*"

Again and again I am asked, "Is divorce and remarriage an unpardonable sin? Is there no forgiveness?" The true question they are asking is, "Can't I stay where I am, and be forgiven?" **Divorce and remarriage is not unforgivable**, but it is important that we understand **true biblical forgiveness**.

I. Biblical Forgiveness: Secured Through Confession, Repentance and Forsaking.

Psalms 32:1,2

"Blessed is the man whose transgression is forgiven, whose sin is covered (paid for). *Blessed is the man unto whom the Lord imputeth not iniquity, and in whose spirit there is no guile."*

Matthew 5:8

"Blessed are the pure in heart: for they shall see God..."

Although these verses seem to be very different in content and social environment, they are very closely tied together in God's scheme of working with man.

Whenever we speak of forgiveness, in the context of the Bible, we must see it in a balanced form.

The blessedness, described here by David and Jesus, only belongs to those who have sincerely turned to God in repentance, and committed their life, without reservation, to the Lordship of Jesus Christ; believing that they have been cleared of all their sin, through his precious blood.

For many today, their confidence of salvation and total forgiveness, is based upon "only believing." As wonderful as that may sound, it manifests an ignorance of Scripture, and a very cheapening view of the incredible work of Christ's atonement. Genuine biblical forgiveness, involves the forgiveness of all sins. The very fact that a man senses a desperate need for forgiveness, implies that he is aware, that sin is defiling, dirty and deadly. We also know, that our God is so holy and righteous, that we cannot truly look to Him without guilt and unworthiness, unless all that defiling, dirty, deadly sin, is dealt with once and for all, through Christ's provisions on Calvary.

The blessedness, spoken of in Pslam 32, does not describe a sinless person; but one who **was defiled** and dirty; **"who has confessed his sin to God, repented of it, and thus obtained forgiveness for all his sin**." By this means, God justifies the ungodly, not on his own works or merit, but totally on the basis of Christ's atoning work. The true balance to this truth, is that a holy God cannot, and will not permit a defiled soul to commune with Him, unless his sin is purged. Pslam 66:18 says:

Psalm 66:18

"If I regard iniquity in my heart, the Lord will not hear me." **The Living Bible** says: *"He would not have listened if I had not confessed my sins."*

Finis J. Dake, in his Annotated Reference Bible says, concerning this verse:

"If I had seen iniquity in my heart and encouraged it; if I had pretended to be what I was not; and if I had loved iniquity while I professed to pray and be sorry for my sin, the Lord...would not have heard me. I would have been left without his help and support in my time of trouble. The first rule of forgiveness is to confess, repent of and forsake all of our past sin. When one is cleansed and forgiven, the Bible speaks of that person as one who is *'pure in heart.'* He has judged himself and his sins in the presence of God, openly, freely, and has no need of covering his transgressions. This one is **'walking in the light**.'"[19]

I John 1:5-10

"This then is the message which we have heard of him, and declare unto you, that God is light, and in him is no darkness at all. If we say that we have fellowship with him,

---

[19]Finis J. Dake, <u>Dake's Annotated Reference Bible</u>, Dake Bible Sales, Inc. Lawrenceville, Georgia. Used by permission.

and walk in darkness, we lie, and do not the truth: But if we walk in the light, as he is in the light, we have fellowship one with another, and the blood of Jesus Christ his Son cleanseth us from all sin. If we say that we have not sin, we deceive ourselves, and the truth is not in us. If we confess our sins, he is faithful and just to forgive us our sins, and to cleanse us from all unrighteousness. If we say that we have not sinned, we make him a liar, and his word is not in us."

This, is **the process** of forgiveness, **the product** of forgiveness, and **the principles** involved in forgiveness. *"God is light, and in him is no darkness at all."* If we are truly forgiven and redeemed by Jesus Christ, we cannot continue to walk in darkness, and say we are in him. Peter tells us about the marvelous change that takes place, in the life of one who has been forgiven.

I Peter 2:9-12

"But ye are a chosen generation, a royal priesthood, an holy nation, a peculiar people; that ye should shew forth the praises of him who hath called you out of darkness into his marvelous light: Which in time past were not a people, but are now the people of God: which had not obtained mercy, but now have obtained mercy. Dearly beloved, I beseech you as strangers and pilgrims, abstain from fleshly lusts, which war against the soul: Having your conversation honest among the Gentiles: that, whereas they speak against you as evildoers, they may by your good works, which they behold, glorify God in the day of visitation."

We suddenly find, that we are in complete opposition to the world system. We love Jesus Christ, and declare him as God of Very God; the Creator, Redeemer, Alpha and Omega, Lord of Lords, King of Kings. We submit to His word, His will, His way. Our appetites, desires, goals, aspirations, purposes, motives, are all in stark contrast to the world system. We march to a new drum beat; we follow a different King, and declare we are pilgrims passing through; ambassadors of a heavenly kingdom. All of this, is the result of knowing we have been forgiven. Unbelievers walk in darkness and refuse to come to the light, while **we desire to walk in the light,** because we have been forgiven.

If, however, one sees no need to confess, repent, and forsake his past sins, then, regardless of our religiosity, fervency, and excitement, *"The truth is not in us."* These poor souls who do not see the awfulness of sin, and still feel they can approach God, by a means other than repentance and forsaking of their past sins, are self-deceived.

I John 1:6

"If we say we have fellowship with him, and walk in darkness, we lie, and do not the truth."

The Amplified Bible says:

"So, if we say we are partakers together and enjoy fellowship with him, when we live and move and are walking around in darkness, We are (both) *speaking falsely and do not live and practice the truth* (of the Gospel).*"*

It is saying, that a person who is truly forgiven, is single minded, and thus walks in a straight path, desiring to please the one who purchased him with his precious blood. If one who is forgiven, stumbles and falls, he should confess it (agree with what God calls it) immediately.

I John 1:9

"If we confess our sins, he is faithful and just to forgive us our sins, and to cleanse us from all unrighteousness."

We are to judge our sin, for what it really is.

I Corinthians 11:31

"For if we would judge ourselves, we should not be judged."

I remember many years ago, when a married woman, with a grown family, came to me for counselling, acting very nervous. This woman, who professed to be a born-again Christian, had been struggling with a serious problem for years. She said she had to get something off her mind, so she could get some peace. She then told me, that she had been having an "ongoing affair," with one of her husband's friends, down the street, for over five years, and knew it had to stop. "What should I do?" she asked.

I said, "First of all, if you feel it is sin, confess it to God, and repent of it."

"What should I say?" she asked.

"Just tell God you have been an adulteress, and you're sorry. Tell him you want to be set free from it, through the blood of Jesus Christ."

She immediately sat up straight, and very defensively said, "I'm not an adulteress, I just had an affair." Then she stopped, dropped her head, and became very quiet for several seconds. When she looked up again, there were tears running down her cheeks, and she said, "Oh my God, I **have been** an adulteress, **I am an adulteress**. I am so sorry, Lord. What an awful sin it is. How blind I have been; please forgive me and set me free. I am sorry; please forgive me, wash me, set me free."

That woman left, a new person, because she got honest with God, judged herself realistically, and knew that, *"The blood of Jesus Christ, His son cleansed her from all sin."* She was totally forgiven, through confession, repentance and forsaking of her sin.

II. Biblical Forgiveness: Secured Through Forgiving Others.

Another biblical truth concerning forgiveness, is that it is reciprocal. If we expect God to forgive us our sins, we are commanded to forgive all others also. The principle is: if you forgive, He will forgive. If you don't forgive, He won't forgive. In fact, **to the degree** that you forgive others, **God will forgive you**. There are many verses that set forth this proposition, and we must recognize, that God is very serious about us being willing to completely forgive others, that we might be forgiven.

In Matthew 6, Jesus was giving his sermon on the mount, where he expounded this vital principle.

Matthew 6:12, 14, 15

"Forgive us our debt, as we forgive our debtors...For if ye forgive men their trespasses, your heavenly Father will also forgive you: But if ye forgive not men their trespasses, neither will your Father forgive your trespasses."

In Luke 11, Jesus's disciples asked him how to pray. He gave them a model prayer which reaffirmed this vital truth again.

Luke 11:4

"And forgive us our sins; for we also forgive every one that is indebted to us..."

Then, in Matthew 18, Jesus uses a striking illustration, not only to teach this principle, but to warn us of the serious consequences, if we fail to obey it.

Matthew 18:21-35

"Then came Peter to him, and said, Lord, how oft shall my brother sin against me, and I forgive him? till seven times? Jesus saith unto him, I say not unto thee, Until seven

times: but, Until seventy times seven. Therefore is the Kingdom of heaven likened unto a certain king, which would take account of his servants. And when he had begun to reckon, one was brought unto him which owed him ten thousand talents. But forasmuch as he had not to pay, his lord commanded him to be sold, and his wife, and children, and all that he had, and payment to be made. The servant therefore fell down, and worshipped him, saying, Lord, have patience with me, and I will pay thee all. Then the lord of that servant was moved with compassion, and loosed him, and forgave him the debt. But the same servant went out and found one of his fellow servants, which owed him an hundred pence: and he laid hands on him and took him by the throat, saying, Pay me that thou owest. And his fellow servant fell down at his feet, and besought him, saying, Have patience with me, and I will pay thee all. And he would not: but went and cast him into prison, till he should pay the debt. So when his fellow servants saw what was done, they were very sorry, and came and told unto their lord all that was done. Then his lord, after that he had called him, said unto him, O thou wicked servant, I forgave thee all that debt, because thou desiredest me: Shouldest not thou also have had compassion on thy fellow servant, even as I had pity on thee? And his lord was wroth, and delivered him to the tormentors, till he should pay all that was due unto him. So likewise shall my heavenly Father do also unto you, if ye from your hearts forgive not everyone his brother their trespasses."

There are many in the church today, who wonder why they have no joy, peace, or lasting satisfaction; who, somewhere along the way, have refused to forgive someone, who has done horrible things to them; or to forgive someone they have loved. Many times they say, "I can't forgive them. You have no idea how I have been hurt by them."

I then, must reiterate this principle of being forgiven, by forgiving others. I show them that they are *"the servant,"* in the illustration, who owed the king somewhere between twelve and twenty million dollars. Like that servant, they possessed no means to pay him; Yet He forgave them completely. Likewise, we are now the servant, who has someone owing us (one days wages) *"an hundred pence;"* and we are saying I can't forgive them.

Please know that I want to say this as lovingly as possible; but I must speak the truth. It really isn't true that we "can't forgive" another person. To make that statement, is a direct contradiction to what Jesus told us to do. In reality, we are really saying, "I will not forgive," and that is rebellion. The Lord Jesus described what the end result of that rebellion would be, in verse 34. And his *"Lord was wroth, and delivered him to the tormentors; till he should pay all that was owed unto him. So likewise shall my heavenly Father do also unto you, if ye from your hearts forgive not everyone his brother their trespasses."*

This is a clear, concise commandment, from Jesus Christ himself, who also said, in John 14:

John 14:45
"If ye love me, keep my commandments."

I am so glad for the degree of forgiveness I received, the night I trusted Christ and repented of my sin.

In Isaiah 38:17, I am told concerning my sins:
"For thou hast cast all my sins behind thy back."

In Micah 7:19b, Micah says of God:
"Thou wilt cast all their sins into the depths of the sea."

In Jeremiah, the Lord is speaking about Israel's sins:

Jeremiah 31:34b
*"...For I will forgive their iniquity and **I will remember their sins no more**."*

The Living Bible says:
"I will forgive and forget their sins."

In Isaiah 43, God is again speaking to Israel and Judah.

Isaiah 43:25
"I, even I, am he that blotteth out thy transgressions for mine own sake, and will not remember thy sins."

In Psalm 103, David declares the extent of our forgiveness:

Pslam 103:12
"As for as the east is from the west, so far hath he removed our transgressions from us."

When God forgave me, he cast my sins *"behind His back,"* into the sea of His forgetfulness, never to be remembered again. They are gone, and He never reminds me of them again (the devil does); never gets historical, when He fellowships with me; never buries the hatchet with the handle sticking out, for future reference. What a Glorious Savior!

One thing that grieves God's heart in this area of forgiveness, is that we expect Him to forgive us completely, to forget all our past transgressions, while we keep giving excuses as to why we can't. No one has nailed us physically to a cross, but they did it to Jesus; and while they were doing it, he was saying, *"Father forgive them."*

Some reading this book, have been wounded terribly by their marriage partner. They have been humiliated, belittled, degraded, cheated on, lied to and abandoned. Yet, **none of these circumstances** excuse us from the obligation of obeying Christ's command to forgive, *"even as God for Christ's sake hath forgiven you."* (Ephesians 4:32)

We must **decide to obey God,** and renounce all the hurt, the anger, the resentment, the self pity, the loneliness, and realize we must forgive them completely; not for their sake, but ours.

I have had so many people say, "I've forgiven them, but I cannot forget it." "...even as God for Christ's sake hath forgiven you." (Ephesians 4:32)

Others have said, "I've forgiven him/her, but I just don't want to be around them anymore; I don't love them anymore."

I wish I could help people to understand that the "love" they once felt, may not be there anymore, because they **changed their minds.** Many say, they have "no feelings for them anymore." Please understand that **love is not a feeling** (although it can produce feelings). **Love is a decision,** that we must make, out of obedience to Christ, whether we feel like it or not. How else could we obey other commands, like:

Matthew 5:43, 45a

"Ye have heard that it hath been said, Thou shalt love thy neighbor, and hate thine enemy. But I say unto you, (This is a command), **love your enemies,** *bless them that curse you, do good to them that hate you, and pray for them that despitefully use you and persecute you; that ye may be children of your Father which is in heaven:...."*

Do you know anyone like that?

Matthew 5:46, 47

"For if ye love them which love you, what reward have ye? do not even the publicans the same? And if ye salute (are friendly to - Living Bible) your brethren only, what do ye more than others? do not even the publicans so?"

208

I was privileged several years ago, to receive a letter from a dear sister, who had purchased four books from our ministry. The letter, was a report, of the results of her handing the books out to some of her friends. Three of the couples had been divorced, irreconcilable, and hardly on speaking terms. This dear sister, went to each of these couples, and asked them to do her only one favor; "Just read this book. That's all I ask." She reported that as the couples read the book, the Lord convicted them of their unforgiving, rebellion spirits. The praise report said, that all three couples repented before God, forgave their partner *"even as God for Christ's sake"* forgave them, and were themselves forgiven. When she sent the letter, all three couples had renewed their vows and were back in church. **Love is a decision**! To forgive is a decision! We must forgive, if we ever hope to be forgiven.

I want each hurting person, to pray about this truth, and then, as an act of your will, obey. Trust may not yet be complete, but start with complete forgiveness, that you might be free. That is so much better than to be *"handed over to the tormentors."*

John 8:36

"If the son, therefore, shall make you free, ye shall be free indeed."

Free through confession, repentance, and the forsaking of all our sins. Free through forgiving others, and escaping *"the tormentors."* This is freedom at it's finest!

Colossians 3:13

*"Forbearing one another, and forgiving one another, is any man have a quarrel against any: **even as Christ forgave you**, so also do ye."*

I Peter 3:9

"Not rendering evil for evil, or railing for railing: but contrariwise blessing; knowing that ye are thereunto called, that ye should inherit a blessing."

May each of us, determine to know the blessing and peace of God, through complete forgiveness. Don't let another day go by; **do it now**!

Section IV

Author's Post Script and
Additional Insights

Chapter 9

Conclusion

Let me share with you, **my reasons for writing this book**. **It was not** because I'm a sadist, or enjoy making waves. Rather:

1. I believe it is a message, that desperately needs to be heard. The moral decline in our nation is unprecedented. These claims of decline, are not being made by the church only, but by secular journalists as well.

As a called servant of Jesus Christ, I believe it's my responsibility to proclaim God's Word, as revealed to me, **even if it isn't popular**. In Acts, Chapter 26, Paul the Apostle, very carefully and clearly, recorded the words which Jesus spoke to him, on the road to Damascus, describing the purpose and scope of Paul's upcoming ministry.

Acts 26:18 (The Living Bible)
*"To open their eyes to their **true condition** so that they may **repent** and live in the light of God instead of in Satan's darkness, so that they may **receive forgiveness** for their sins and **God's inheritance** along with all people everywhere whose sins are cleansed away, who are set apart by faith in Me (Jesus)."*

2. **Another reason I wrote this book, was my desire is to be faithful to my calling,** which includes, **warning our young people of teachings and practices contrary to God's Word.** I realize this message may be discouraging for some already involved in the difficult entanglements of adultery. However, if this message should cause young people to **reassess their motivations** for marriage, and if it will help them to realize **the permanency of that decision,** then it will have been worth it all.

Young people are marrying for many wrong reasons today.

☞   **To get even with parents**—This attitude is rooted in rebellion, and doomed to failure.

☞   **To escape from home responsibilities**—"When I get married, I won't have to do dishes, cook, iron, mow lawns, and I can be my own boss, etc."

☞   **Fear of losing out**—"Everyone else I went to school with is getting married. I don't want to be the only one left, single. After all I'm almost nineteen."

☞   **Physical attraction**—Young people need to realize that physical beauty and popularity are fleeting things, and that while in school, developing skills and talents for the future, should become their first priority. When seeking a life's partner they should look beyond the shallowness of physical beauty and popularity, and seek one who also is preparing for better things in the future. They need to know that the marriage relationship is **for life—go slowly!**

3. This book has been written, to encourage married couples to work harder at maintaining their marriage relationships.

Since preaching this message for the first time more than twenty years ago, I've been privileged to counsel many couples with **irreconcilable problems**. When the ones I counselled were genuine Christians, and they learned that Jesus taught marriage was for life, their irreconcilable problems were not only reconcilable; but by rebuilding the new relationship upon a solid Scriptural foundation, a new and exciting love and respect was experienced toward each other.

One close friend of ours called one day, to say she had a sister and brother-in-law who were separated, and heading for divorce. "If my sister came down, would you share with her what God's Word says?" my friend asked. Her sister did fly down, and spent about two hours asking questions. With a set of tapes in her hand, she went back North, where she and her husband sat down, opened their Bibles, and studied the tapes together. The impossible, became possible, and they reunited. The last I heard, they were back in church serving, the Lord together.

Several years ago, a member of my former fellowship, had a friend from the North visit, during a Christian retreat. She had been divorced for about five years, and saw no chance of, or desire to reconcile. This member called one afternoon, and asked if I'd come over. We spent several hours studying what the Word of God says about marriage and divorce. Some months later, I heard that they had reconciled, and were happily back together.

One of the greatest problems one must confront in a divorce situation, is **unforgiveness**. Let me quickly say again, that when a person says, **"I can't forgive,"** he or she is actually saying **"I won't forgive." Forgiveness is not an emotion**. It is an **act of the will**.

The experiences and trials of marriage, are **for our benefit**. They function like a pressure cooker, designed by God, to bring about change, growth, maturity, and the ability to bear responsibility.

I've heard marriage partners say, "You don't know what he or she does to me. Every time he/she gets around me, I go crazy." Just remember, he/she can **only stir up** what is already **in you!**

A well known pastor, while speaking at a Jesus Rally, in Florida, many years ago, gave a powerful illustration of this truth that I hope I'll never forget. He held a glass of cola in his hand. Then he called a young man up onto the platform. He asked the young man to grip the forearm of the hand holding the cola, and then to shake it. "Harder," he said. Suddenly the cola was spilling onto the platform. "What made the cola spill?" he asked.

"I shook your arm," replied the young man.

"Oh no," he said, "The cola spilled, **because that's what was in the glass**. If there were milk in the glass, I would have spilled milk. If there were water in the glass, I would have spilled water. The shaking, **only spills what is in the cup.**" Your partner, only causes, or caused to spill out of you, what's **already there!** If you didn't have anger in you, it couldn't spill out.

The same speaker also said, "A beautiful girl walking by, doesn't **make you lust**. Her passing by, just shows you that **lust is operating inside of you**, and you need to let God deal with it."

What was displayed, when your wife or husband **shook you**? Remember, the Lord only **used them,** to reveal to you, what was in you, and needed to be dealt with. Your running away from that situation solved nothing. Just because you're away from them, doesn't mean that it's not there now. That anger, lust, jealously, or hatred in you, or me, is just waiting for someone else to come along and shake us enough, to make it manifest itself again—to let you see, that the problem you thought you had run away from, is still there. You see, God knew that if He let your **parents** point it out to you, you could just leave home, instead of changing. If your **boss** exposes the anger in you, you can quit. But when you became *"one flesh,"* **for life,** with someone, the Lord knew He would have time to work on that inward problem—**unless** you choose to violate His **universal marriage law**. God wants to use the marriage relationship, to deal with the inward problems you may have, and to mold you into the image of Christ. **Let Him do it!**

4. Another reason for this book is to warn everyone as lovingly as I can, not to be deceived, concerning adultery. Paul, in I Corinthians, Chapter 6, gives us a stern warning concerning it.

> **I Corinthians 6:9-10**
> *"...adulterers...shall* **(not)** *inherit the kingdom of God."*

If you say, "I feel my divorce and subsequent marriages have nothing to do with my salvation," you must remember that what you think or feel, does not affect or change the clear, teaching of the word of God. You must examine what you think and feel, in the light of what God said, and submit to the truthfulness and authority of that which was spoken by our Lord Jesus. Jesus said, *"My sheep hear my voice, and they follow me."* If Jesus said you are *"one flesh"* **for life**, and you have divorced and married again, **you have not heard His voice**, but instead, have **disobeyed His direct command**. **Jesus said,** a person who divorces and marries another person, is an **adulterer**, and

Paul said, *"...adulterers shall* (not) *inherit the kingdom of God."*

When, or if, you say that divorce and subsequent marriages have nothing to do with your salvation, I am forced to make a very difficult decision. Do I trust in **your** "**experience**," in **your conviction,** in what **you say**; or do I believe **the eternal word of God**? Jesus said; in John; Chapter 12:

> **John 12:48**
> *"He that rejecteth me, and receiveth not my words, hath one that judgeth him: the words that I have spoken, the same shall judge him in the last day."*

Notice, **it doesn't say,** the words that **Shammai** has spoken, or the words that **Moses** has spoken, will judge you. It says, *"The words that **I have spoken**, the same shall judge him in the last day."*

When Jesus was on the Mount of Transfiguration, with Peter, James, and John, a bright cloud appeared over them. In Matthew, Chapter 17, it says:

> **Matthew 17:5**
> *"and behold a voice **out of the cloud**, which said, This is my beloved Son, in whom I am well pleased; hear ye him."*

That clearly tells you who was speaking? There is no higher source. **You have heard from the chairman of the board—the final authority.**

You and I, must refuse to put confidence in **any experience or feeling,** that is in conflict with **the Word**. Our Heavenly Father said:

Matthew 17:5

"...*This is my beloved Son, in whom I am well pleased; hear ye him.*" (**Not,** hear an **experience**. **Not,** hear a **preacher**. **Not,** hear another **author,** but "*hear ye him.*" **Don't be deceived about adultery.**)

5. I have written this book, to faithfully declare the message the Lord put into my heart, and told me to preach. I have held back nothing, out of fear of what men might think or say. Consequently, I feel, I have been totally obedient, and can say concerning this word which the Lord has called me to declare; that which the Apostle Paul said in Acts, Chapter 20.

Acts 20:26-32

"*Wherefore I take you to record this day, that I am pure from the blood of all men. For I have not shunned to declare unto you all the counsel of God. Take heed therefore unto yourselves, and to all the flock, over the which the Holy Ghost hath made you overseers, To feed the church of God, which he hath purchased with his own blood. For I know this, that after my departing shall grievous wolves enter in among you not sparing the flock. Also of your own selves shall men arise, speaking perverse things to draw away disciples after them. Therefore watch, and remember, that by the space of three years I ceased not to warn every one night and day with tears. And now brethren, I commend you unto God, and to the word of his grace, which is able to build you up, and to give you an inheritance among all them which are sanctified.*"

May this counsel be used by the Holy Spirit, to cause men and women **to go back to the Scriptures,** with open hearts and minds, **to hear** *"what the Spirit saith unto the churches. "* Revelation 2:29.

So many times people have said to me, "Brother, I see it; what shall I do now? Should I leave the one I'm living with now, or what?"

I will tell **you,** what I have to tell **them.** **"I did not create the problem you're in, and I shall not advise you what steps to take. I have told you what the Word of God says. If the Holy Spirit bears witness in your heart that it is truth; then I encourage you, as Mary did the servants at the marriage at Cana, when she sent them to Jesus, in John, Chapter 2."** She declared:

John 2:5
> *"Whatsoever he saith unto you, do it."*

I know that **whatever the Holy Spirit says,** will be **totally consistent with the Word.**

My prayer is, that somehow, my God will use this book, to cause God's people to declare to the world, that **"marriage is, till death do us part."**

If anyone knows they are living in sin and disobedience, according to the clear teachings of God's word, and **think** they can somehow beat the odds, by **doing nothing about it, they are living in a fantasy world, in willful, scriptural ignorance,** and **rebellion.**

James 4:17
> *"Therefore to him that knoweth to do good, and doeth it not, to him it is sin."*

Again in Numbers, Chapter 32, we read:

Numbers 32:23

"...be sure your sin will find you out."

The end result of **not acting** on this truth is spelled out, in James, Chapter 1.

James 1:15
*"...When **lust** hath conceived, it bringeth forth **sin: and sin,** when it is finished, **bringeth forth death.**"*

Solomon said it just as succinctly is Proverbs Chapter 29.

Proverbs 29:1
*"He, that being often reproved hardeneth his neck, shall **suddenly be destroyed, and that without remedy.**"*

May God the Holy Spirit, help and guide you into *"all truth,"* **and give you the boldness and strength to completely obey the truth you have received.**

So get rid of all uncleanness and the rampant outgrowth of wickedness, and in a humble (gentle, modest) spirit receive and welcome the Word which implanted and rooted [in your hearts] contains the power to save your souls.

But—obey the message; be doers of the Word, and not merely listeners to it, betraying yourselves [into deception by reasoning contrary to the Truth].

James 1:21-22

The Amplified New Testament

Chapter **10**

Questions and Answers

During the past twenty-seven years, I've had questions asked me, concerning other verses of Scripture, or opinions, indirectly related to this subject matter. In trying to answer some of these questions, maybe the answers will tie some loose ends together for you, in your continued search for a Scriptural position.

The first question, referred to Illustration #6. That illustration, depicts Jack and Jill being divorced, and Jack, subsequently, marrying Sue.

QUESTION

If Sue had never been married before she walked the aisle with Jack, what is **her marital status** at this time, if God's Word says their relationship is adulterous? Also, if she and Jack separated, then she got saved, would she have to remain single the rest of her life? This is especially crucial, since, later on, you indicated she and Jack had two children during their relationship.

ANSWER

Follow closely, and I'll try to explain **from the scriptural position,** what took place. When Jack walked the aisle with Sue, he was already, *"one flesh"* with Jill. Therefore, God rejected (refused to act on) Jack and Sue's vows. The vows stated by Jack and Sue, would not be honored by God, anymore than He would honor (or act upon) the vows of two sodomites, a brother and sister, a father and daughter, or mother and son, at an altar, making marriage vows. These are **scripturally forbidden relationships**, and thus unrecognized and unacceptable to the one who originated the marriage, and makes two **one**. **Despite** the marriage certificate **issued by man**, Sue was living in **a state** of *"adultery."* Refer to Illustrations #6 and #7 again. Since **Jack was still married to Jill,** in God's eyes, this relationship constituted adultery (against his wife Jill). Meanwhile, Sue, was still a **single person,** in God's eyes, in spite of her vows to Jack. She was not married in God's eyes because the vows between her and Jack were **forbidden,** and thus, **unrecognized**. Thus, they **could not be made** *"one flesh,"* by a Holy God. See Luke 16:18.

In my first printing, I "coined" a new term, to describe definitively the difference between Jack and Sue's particular transgression. That term was **"single adultery."** By some of the letters I received, you would have thought I had committed the unpardonable sin.

Sometimes, the Scripture only defines **the general violation** of the law. At other times, only one aspect of a violation. This does not mean, that the other definition is invalid. One example, is in Matthew, Chapter 5, where Jesus said:

Matthew 5:28
*"...whosoever looketh on a woman to lust after her **hath committed adultery** (moicheuo) with her already in his heart."*

I completely believe every word of that verse, but also can add, or more precisely define and apply this verse, without denying or violating its truth. For example, if **a single man** looks on **a single woman** and lusts in his heart, can that be **adultery,** when **no covenant vows** have been violated? No! We can call it fornication, but it still violates the 7th commandment, which says, *"Thou shalt not commit adultery."* There is no eleventh commandment that says, **"Thou shalt not commit fornication,"** **but all moral impurity, is implied** in that seventh commandment.

Another example, to show that defining or clarifying Biblical violations is not heresy, is the tenth commandment, which says, *"Thou shalt not covet...thy neighbor's wife."*

Moses calls it *"coveting;"* but it also comes under Jesus' teaching, in Matthew, Chapter 5, where he speaks of *"looking and lusting after a woman,"* and is thus to be considered adultery also. Which one should I call it? In reality, it **is both**. In reality, it is also selfishness, greed, lust, etc.

Therefore, to say scripturally, that Sue committed adultery with Jack is true according to Luke 16:18. But **more definitively,** Jack committed adultery (violating his covenant with his wife Jill), and Sue committed fornication with Jack (illicit sex act by an unmarried person). **Technically,** therefore, one was committing fornication, and the other adultery—"single adultery."

The bottom line however, is that it is **all sin**, and if not repented, of will send a person to hell.

I Corinthians 6:9-10

*"Be not deceived; neither **fornicators**...nor* *adulterers...nor **covetous** shall inherit the kingdom of* *God."*

God, **could not** make Sue *"one flesh"* with Jack. In God's eyes, they were in an illegitimate and unlawful relationship, because Jack was still married to Jill. Thus, Jack and Sue's children were also illegitimate, **in God's eyes**. Again refer to Luke 16:18.

In the event that Sue and Jack **separated**, and since God did not recognize them as being in a *"one flesh"* union, Sue would then have **ceased from living in a state of adultery with Jack**. If Sue would then **repent** of that relationship with Jack, the blood of Jesus would wash that sin away forever. The scars or remembrance of that sin might remain, but the guilt of that sin would be gone (Proverbs 6:32, 33). Sue would, according to God's Word, be as though she had never committed adultery with Jack. Thus, Sue, now forgiven, would be free to marry a widower, or a man who had never before been married and divorced. If Sue had become a Christian, one more stipulation would be included. She could **only** marry another Christian (I Corinthians 7:39).

I counseled a man several years ago, who had walked the aisle, reciting marriage vows with two different women, but still **was not married,** in God's sight. Both women had been married before, to men who had never been married before. Therefore, they, each, were already in a *"one flesh"* relationship, for life, with another man. He, has since, left the second woman. Through repentance, this man could be forgiven of those adulterous relationships, and be free to marry, in accordance with the universal marriage law.

Someone may say, "Man that's the way to go. Just marry formerly married women, and you can get out of it." I will remind you, that *"fornicators…shall not inherit the kingdom of God"* either. *"Whatsoever a man soweth that shall he also reap,"* is another **universal law**.

QUESTION

If God hates divorce so much, why did Jesus forgive the woman **caught in the very act of adultery,** when the others wanted to stone her? (John 8:4-11)

ANSWER

Please understand! **God hates sin;** but **loves the sinner!** If we are truly saved, then so should we hate sin. Paul emphasized this truth, in Romans, Chapter 5.

> ### Romans 5:8
> *"But God commandeth his love toward us, in that while we were yet sinners, Christ died for us."*

When the woman was brought to Jesus; (It is interesting to note that they only brought the woman.) Jesus sensed something in her, that caused him to say, in John, Chapter 8:

> ### John 8:11
> *"Neither do I condemn thee..."*

This is one portion of Scripture, that so many try to camp out on. This is the one verse, they love to recite to me over and over. This verse, gives them great comfort, in their sin. Their security and comfort is **unfounded**, however, whenever the whole verse is read; **so please**—don't stop reading there! That's a **colon, not a period.** He's not through yet. Her forgiveness, was pronounced with the following command. *"Go and sin no more."* This is what Jesus says to all of us, *"repent."* That is, to change our mind 180 degrees, to where you now abhor and hate your sin, enough to **forsake it.** Then, and only then, is his forgiveness ours—full and complete.

QUESTION

How about David and Bathsheba? David committed adultery with Bathsheba, and later on married her. Solomon, their son, became the next king of Israel. Weren't they living in adultery? If so, how could God bless the offspring of this relationship?

ANSWER

This question has come up many times. First, realize we are examining **Old Testament morality,** which we are told, in Acts 17:30, God *"let slide."* Examples of this overlooking of immorality are many in the Old Testament, including the Psalmist who had several wives. Again, it is evident, when we see that David committed an **act of adultery,** and then **murder**. Psalm 51, is evidence of David's acknowledging his sins, and of his genuine repentance for them.

In spite of his repentance, David, his nation, and his whole family, suffered greatly for his disobedience. To understand their relationship, we must realize, that Bathsheba's husband was now dead, through David's scheming. **Bathsheba was a widow. And thus, she was eligible to marry David, according to the then prevailing Old Testament Theology.** But let it be noted, that David disobeyed another commandment of God, by marrying her. In Deuteronomy 17:17, God established a higher law, which said of the king:

Deuteronomy 17:17
"Neither shall he multiply wives to himself, that his heart turn not away;"

David married her, and Solomon was born into a socially **legitimate, but scripturally disobedient home**. God completely forgave David's sins of murder and adultery after his repentance, but David's family and nation, paid a terrible price. Thus, **David and Bathsheba's marriage, by the then prevailing Old Testament standard, although disobedience, was not adulterous.** I've had people say to me "That's the answer; I'll go back and **kill my former partner**, and then I can stay with this

228

one." I'll only suggest that you read of David's punishment first. Know also, what the Apostle John said, in I John, Chapter 3, and Revelation, Chapter 20.

I John 3:15b

*"ye know that **no murderer** hath eternal life abiding in him."*

Revelation 21:8

*"...**murderers**...shall have their part in the lake which burneth with fire and brimstone: which is the **second death**."*

It is amazing to me, how man tries to get around God's way, when God's way is always best.

It has been said, that society has enacted over ten thousand laws, to get men to obey God's ten commandments, and men are still finding loopholes. How true were the words of Jeremiah, in Chapter 17.

Jeremiah 17:9

"The heart is deceitful above all things and desperately wicked: who can know it?"

Let me bring out one other point, while we are on the subject of David and Bathsheba. There are those who will tell you, that sex between a man and a woman makes them *"one flesh."* Here, we find that David committed adultery with Bathsheba, resulting in her getting pregnant, while her husband was gone to war. There isn't even a **hint** that David and Bathsheba were made, or became *"one flesh,"* as a result of that sin. In fact, after David repented, he then married Bathsheba, and consequently **became** *"one flesh"* with her. Here again we see that the sex act between a man and a woman, does not make the two *"one flesh."*

QUESTION

Doesn't I Corinthians 7:9 say, God doesn't want us to remain unmarried, if we *"burn?"*

ANSWER

I Corinthians 7:9, should not be read without I Corinthians 7:8. When you seek "proof texts," you can get into trouble. Paul is only speaking of two specific classes of people here.

I Corinthians 7:8

*"I say therefore to the **unmarried** (never married) and **widows**, (those whose marriage partners have died) it is good for them if they abide even as I. But if they cannot contain, **let them marry**: for it is better to marry than to burn."*

This is **not** God's endorsement of multiple marriages or progressive polygamy. God, wants those burnings met, through a Biblically approved marriage. That burning, may be the area of life an individual needs to go back and seek godly counseling about, but it **does not** give a divorced person permission or encouragement to marry another spouse. It **only** applies to those **never married,** or those whose **first marriage partner has died** and the surviving partner has needs, that can only be scripturally met, in a marriage relationship.

QUESTION

I believe, I Corinthians 7:20 tells me, that if I am divorced and have married a second, or third partner, and then become a Christian, I should not change my status, but rather:

I Corinthians 7:20

"Let every man abide in the same calling wherein he was called."

ANSWER

Again, it is impossible to take a Scripture verse out of context, and arrive at a **sound** solution. I Corinthians 7:20-24, is speaking to a society that had a **caste system**. If your father was a slave, so were you. Some of the saints that were slaves, wanted to know if they should revolt. To them, Paul said, "No, stay there, because, even as a slave, you are free in Jesus Christ."

The **folly** of such a doctrinal position as you suggest is obvious, if we apply it to **any other sinful situations**. Paul was not saying to the **alcoholic,** "If Christ calls you to himself as an alcoholic, and saves you, remain an alcoholic." To the **pimp,** he wouldn't say, "Keep your business going." Paul wouldn't tell a **sodomite,** "Stay where you are"? How about a thief? The Ten Commandments say, *"Thou shalt not steal."* Can I tell a **thief** to keep on stealing?

Are these situations any different? No, they're not. The only reason they seem different, is because we are judging them according to present-day-societal norms, instead of God's Holy Word. I Corinthians 6:9-10, names each of these lifestyles, along with adultery, as sins, which if not repented of, will send a man to hell. Therefore, if this proposition cannot be applied to these other lifestyles, it cannot be applied to people who have divorced and married other spouses.

QUESTION

You keep saying that a person cannot get free from their partner, or marry another person, while their first spouse is living. Please explain to me I Corinthians 7:27, which says in the King James Version:

I Corinthians 7:27

"Art thou bound unto a wife? seek not to be loosed. Art thou loosed from a wife? seek not a wife."

What does it mean to be **loosed** or to be **bound**?

ANSWER

I am so glad you brought up this verse, because many have felt that **this** verse, invalidates the whole argument, presented in this book. But again let me say, **doctrine is not established by unclear** verses, but by the **clear ones**.

Note first of all that Paul, in verse 25, is speaking to "**virgins**." In verse 26, Paul says, because of the difficult times of that day, it is better to remain unmarried and a virgin.

In verse 27, Paul begins a new thought. We must realize that Paul was not writing a term paper, but a **letter**. Because it was a letter, he took the freedom to write about problems as they came to him. Verse 27, if interpreted properly, will **agree** with **all other clear verses**, and consistently support the same message found throughout Scripture.

Paul, was establishing New Testament conduct in the early church. In verse 27, one Scripturally consistent possibility would be that he was confronting the Old Testament teaching of Deuteronomy 24:1-4, concerning the *"putting away of wives."*

Paul taught Timothy that he was not to appoint any man to the office of a deacon or bishop, unless they were, *"The husband of one wife."* Many, evidently, coming from the old system, were coming into the Church, carrying with them the now obsolete Old Testament Mosaic system of binding and loosing themselves from their wives. Paul, therefore, was saying, "Those of you who have come into the Church, having practiced the old Mosaic Principle, must realize that the **old way is over**." If you are presently *"**bound** or glued unto a wife,"*, don't ever again seek *"to be **loosed**"*. Again, if you are now separated from your wife and are seeking a new one, **stop it now**. That Old Testament principle no longer applies. **Complete truth has come!**

Another scripturally consistent, but problematic possibility, was that Paul was still speaking to **singles,** who were **engaged,** or had been divorced from an **engagement**. To believe this we would have to assume the term, *"wife,"* was applied here as it was when Jesus used it, in Matthew 1:20, 24. Then it would be saying to the **singles**, "Because of the difficult times we are in today, it's more prudent to stay single. In saying this, I am not telling you to abandon any present commitments. If you are engaged to a *'wife,'* don't seek to loose her. If you have broken your engagement through divorce, don't get involved again with another during these chaotic times." This again, would be consistent and contextually correct.

When Paul gets to verse 28, he is speaking to **virgins** again. It is to them, he says, *"If you marry, you have not sinned."* I am **amazed,** that some Bible teachers today, try to apply this verse to **divorced people**.

To show you that Paul was **only** speaking to **virgins** in verse 28, look at verse 36 of the same Chapter, and you will see the same phrase, used again, referring specifically to **virgins**.

I Corinthians 7:36
*"But if any man think that he behaveth himself uncomely toward his virgin, if she pass the flower of her age, and need so require, let him do what he will, **he sinneth not: let them marry**."*

Here, we have the same phrase as is found, in verse 28, that some would **love** to make apply to **divorced** persons. If it **did** refer to divorcees, then this one **obscure verse,** would **make void** all the **clear verses,** and **contradict** all the **clear teaching** in God's Word. Rather than weaken, this portion reconfirms, that God's truths and principles have never changed. Our Lord Jesus, firmly **reestablished** God's original, unchanging standard for the marriage, and the Apostle Paul was confirming it here, to the Corinthian Church, by instructing this certain group as to what the Biblical parameters of their situation were.

QUESTION

How can you say that God doesn't recognize divorce, when in John, Chapter 4, Jesus was talking to the Samaritan woman at the well, and told her:

John 4:18
"For thou hast had five husbands; and he whom thou now hast is not thy husband:"

ANSWER

As you look at the woman of Samaria at the well, you are looking at two possibilities. The first possibility, is that this woman had experienced widowhood five times, and was now living with a man, though not married to him. The second possibility is that we are looking at the end result of Moses' concession in Deuteronomy 24:1-4. What Jesus said to her, was Deuteronomy 24 in operation. This woman, had evidently received five "bills of divorcement" from the five men. She had married these men under what I'd like to term "the concession for the hard-hearted," by Moses. After being rejected five times, she had gotten tired of all the paperwork involved in the marriage law, and tried what many think is a New Morality idea. She was now living with her sixth partner, but on a trial basis, before they committed themselves to marriage. Consequently, we find a woman being isolated by the people of Sychar. She didn't even come for water with the rest of the women of the city in the cool of the morning or evening, as was the custom, but had come alone, at (midday), the sixth hour.

Jesus spoke the truth to this woman. Under **the old agreement,** established by Moses, **up to her last relationship**, she had been functioning according to the moral code of her day.

When you see the moral morass this system brought, it's no wonder Paul, by divine revelation, said that **pastors**, **elders**, **bishops**, and **deacons** must be literally *"one-woman men."* God's original standard was now being reestablished, *"wherein dwelleth righteousness."* (II Peter 3:13b)

Jesus, therefore, was not approving this woman's immorality. He simply let her know that he knew all things. Divorced persons, and those who have married again after divorcing, will never, with textual honesty, draw comfort from this portion of Scripture again. The New Covenant, strictly **forbids** such lifestyles for those living today, **if** they intend to go to Heaven.

Here again, we also see how sex does not make a *"one flesh"* relationship by itself. Jesus said, that although this woman was **living** with this man, like he was her husband, he still **wasn't** her husband. Thus, their sexual relationships, **did not** result in a *"one flesh"* relationship.

QUESTION

Doesn't I Corinthians 6:16, indicate that having sex with a harlot, does cause a one flesh relationship, and therefore, is a direct contradiction to your teaching?

ANSWER

Without going into a lengthy dissertation, let me encourage you to do a word study of this portion of Scripture. When you do, you will find that it will actually agree with, and strengthen my arguments. The first word to note is the word *"joined."* The Greek word is **kollaomai**, which means glued, cemented, or permanently bound. This implies more than a one time affair.

Then, Paul goes on to explain his source for this truth. *"For two saith he, shall be one flesh."*

Who is the "he"? Who said "...two...shall be one flesh"?

God said it, in Genesis 2:24; and Jesus said it, in Matthew 9:5,6.

What event were God the Father, and Jesus Christ speaking about when they said it? Was it a one night stand? No, they were speaking only of marriage.

Paul was saying, we should not be unequally yoked, but if we do marry, even a harlot, we are joined (glued or cemented) into a one flesh relationship.

Let's look at some scriptural examples, to see if this interpretation is consistent with other portions of the Word.

In reading Genesis 38, you will find that Judah had a sexual encounter with his daughter-in-law, Tamar, who had disguised herself as a harlot. As a result, Tamar became pregnant from that one encounter. Neither Judah, nor Tamar, intimated or suggested that their illicit affair, which resulted in the birth of a child, caused them to be one flesh. In fact, in verse 26, of Genesis 38, it says, *"He knew her no more again."*

When Jesus spoke, in Luke 16:18, he said, *"whosoever divorces his wife and **marries another** commits adultery."* I believe **this type of relationship** would definitely involve sexual relations. He didn't suggest that those sexual relations now make them one flesh, but rather, said they were committing adultery (illicit sex outside the marriage). Paul, in I Corinthian 6:16 is referring to only one possible source, when he declares, *"For two saith he, shall be one flesh."* And that reference confirms a marital joining.

To infer that God's holy process for becoming one flesh (a vow or commitment), could possibly be realized by illegitimate sexual means, would also infer, in verse 17, that Gods holy process of being joined to Christ, as "one spirit," can be realized in a similar illegitimate way. **God forbid!**

QUESTION

In Matthew 19, Jesus was responding to the Pharisees' question concerning marriage and divorce. Why, in verse 11, did he say, *"All men cannot receive this saying, save they to whom it is given"*? Then in the last part of verse 12, he added, *"He that is able to receive it, let him receive it."* Shouldn't these verses let us off the hook, and allow us an escape from what you are teaching?

ANSWER

Here again is a misapplication of clear scriptural teaching, for the sake of obtaining a proof text. When these verses (10-12) are put in their proper context, they only strengthen and reaffirm everything I have said. Verses 11 and 12, are in response, not to verses 3 through 9, where Jesus taught about marriage and divorce, but rather, to the response of the disciples, to Jesus, concerning the new higher standard Jesus had just placed before them. In verse 10, in despair, the disciples said, *"It is not good to marry."*

In reality, Christ's new teaching was so different from anything they had ever heard; so much more binding and permanent, that they almost groaned in shock, *"It is not good to marry."* It was to this, that Jesus responded.

Other well known commentators confirm this fact, that Jesus was responding to what the disciples had just said, and not to what **he** had just taught.

Lenski in his commentary on Matthew says of this portion,

"v. 10 is divided, and only it's last half, 'it is not expedient to marry,' is referred to 'this saying' of which Jesus says that not all have room for it."[20]

Barnes notes on Matthew 19:11, "All men cannot receive this saying. The minds of men are not prepared for this. This saying, evidently means what the disciples had just said - That it was good for a man not to marry."[21]

John A. Broadus D. D. L. L. D. on Matthew, "Our Lord's reply is that marriage is sometimes not expedient. All men cannot receive this saying 'viz'. The saying that is not expedient to marry. What they have said is true in some cases, and for a special reason, quite different from the one intimated by them. To understand 'this saying' as his own saying, that marriage is indissoluble, would make the Savior contradict his own argument, for he had argued from the divine purpose in the creation of man. 'Receive' does not here mean to accept as true, but the peculiar Greek word signifies to have space in one's nature for something - like a vessel holding so much, comp. John 21:25 - sometimes in the sense of capacity to know...here in the sense of capacity to act out. 'Not all men have room (capacity) for this saying.'"[22]

---

[20]Reprinted from INTERPRETATION OF MATTHEW'S GOSPEL by R. C. H. Lenski, copyright© 1937 Lutheran Book Concern. Used by permission of Augsburg Fortress.

[21]Reprinted from Notes on the New Testament by Albert Barnes, copyright 1954. Used by permission of Baker Publishing Company.

[22]Matthew, by John A. Broadus D.D., L. L. D., Copyright 1886, American Baptist Publication Society.

John Monro Gibson MA - D. D. The Gospel of Matthew, Verse 10-12, "The wide prevalence of lax views on this subject is made evident by the perplexity of the disciples. They were not at all prepared for such stringency, so they venture to suggest that if that is to be the law, better not to marry at all. The answer our Lord gives, while it does admit that there are circumstances in which celibacy is preferable, plainly intimates that it is only in quite exceptional cases."[23]

This portion, which you indicate should let you off the hook, cannot even be used against the theme of this book. This portion, as you can clearly see from what I have said, and have confirmed by other scholarly commentators, has absolutely nothing to do with what Jesus taught about the permanency of marriage. Jesus was simply responding to the desperate, squirming statement the disciples uttered, when our "Gracious and loving Lord Jesus Christ," placed God's eternal will concerning the marriage upon them. Jesus said, "it's easy to say you'd rather not marry, but very few have the capacity to live with that. If some desire to remain single, they may, but not all men can live singly."

So, as you can see, your argument is based on a false premise. The teaching of marriage and divorce applies to all men and women, saved or unsaved. They must choose marriage, or the single life, based upon the principles God has established in his Word.

QUESTION

If what you have shown us from the Scriptures is true, why hasn't the Church taught it, and why is divorce and multiple marriages so widespread in the churches themselves?

---

[23] The Gospel of St. Matthew, by John Monro Gibson, MA, D.D., A.C. Armstrong & Son, New York.

ANSWER

What we have seen happen in our churches, has been a gradual change of attitude, that has evolved over a period of many years. It has been said, that backsliding is never a **blowout**, but just a **slow leak**. Several decades ago, the church experienced an influx of couples, who had divorced their first spouses and married again. These couples, had remained with their second or third partners for an extended period of time before they entered the church doors. To make an issue out of their present long-term relationship, therefore, caused much dissent in the churches by well-meaning church-goers. The defenders of these couples, said that the Church should "learn to forgive," and not to treat these unfortunate people as "**second-class citizens**." That term, "**second-class citizens**," became the offensive phrase and buzzword, around which supporters rallied. A real struggle ensued, and no one came forth with a strong doctrinal position on this issue, because it was so volatile. One needs only to examine most commentaries pastors use today, to find that passages dealing with divorce and subsequent marriages, were, and are, virtually skipped over, or very lightly touched upon. You will find, however, the older the commentary, the stronger the teaching.

The result of this compromise in the Church, reads like the parable of the Arab's camel. Remember how the camel stuck his nose in the Arab's tent, and asked, "May I just keep my nose inside the tent, to keep it warm?" When given approval, the camel stuck his whole head into the tent, and asked if it was all right to keep his ears warm, because it was so cold outside. The evident end of the parable was, that inch by inch, the camel moved into the tent, until he was all the way in, and the Arab was out. It happened slowly, but it happened.

Likewise, through compromise and faulty doctrine, the **camel of adultery,** is not only in the tent (the Church), but he has now made it easier for more camels of unrighteousness to enter into the tent (the Church).

It is time, to recognize that divorced people, who have married again, while their first partner is still alive, are not "unfortunate or second-class persons." God's Word says, they are sinners, who at sometime in the past made a decision to, or was advised, to disobey clear Biblical commands. They now need to repent, so that they may receive eternal life. Just because they are in denominational bodies, does not mean they are **in Christ**. The real tragedy, is that they are not only **in** the churches, but occupy very influential offices in the churches, as deacons, trustees, teachers, and pastors.

The Body of Christ must pay a dear price today, if it would get the camel back out of the tent, to reestablish righteousness. Whatever the price, it is worthwhile, to purify the assembly and to enlighten these dear souls of their lost condition, before it's too late.

The Church today, has been deluged with books, trying to **justify,** and even **promote,** the **acceptance of adultery into the Church.** Be assured of this, however, that **judgment will come,** if the Church doesn't repent and purge itself of this condition. In saying that **the true Church must be purged**, it should not be implied that the Church should reject those persons living in sexual immorality, any more than they should reject any other sinner; whether it be murder, stealing, etc. Rather, the Church should declare to them their lost condition, and **remove them from leadership and membership** until they repent. God loves sinners, and we must love them too. Remember, however, that love does not mean approving of, or condoning their condition. Neither does it mean withholding from them their **true condition before God**. Jesus Christ loved you and me, while we were yet in our sins, but he hated our condition. Therefore, he sent the Holy Spirit, to convict us **of our true condition,** that we might repent before it is too late.

This task of cleansing the local assemblies won't come easy; make no mistake of this. The Church today has done to adulterers and adulteresses what Jesus said the Jews did when they recruited proselytes in Matthew Chapter 23.

Matthew 23:15

"Woe unto you, scribes and Pharisees, hypocrites! for ye compass sea and land to make one proselyte, and when he is made, ye make him two fold more the child of hell than yourselves."

Jesus was saying, "Until you Jews salved that sinner's conscience, by making him believe he was all right since he became like you, he could have been reached. But now, it will be next to impossible to reach him, since he is your proselyte, and has been made to feel comfortable in his deception."

Many persons who have divorced, and are now in adulterous relationships, have been accepted as **fellow saints** into the church, and have become satisfied, convinced, and embedded. Why should they believe this truth? They have already been accepted and integrated, and their lifestyle condoned. They are already **"inside the Arab's tent** looking out," and saying, "Why **should** we repent?"

If this message is not preached clearly today, not only will they be lost, without hope, inside the physical framework of what we may call the Church, but the next generation will be like ships without a moral rudder. The Church of Jesus Christ, **dare not wait** another generation to declare this truth. This nation, as we have known it, cannot survive another generation of moral decay, without someone showing them that there is a **God who is**, and who **expects** and **demands righteousness**.

Proverbs 14:34

"Righteousness exalteth a nation: but sin is a reproach to any people."

QUESTION

What should I do if my marriage partner commits adultery?

ANSWER

If you had lived in Old Testament times, the answer to this question would have been, to **stone them**. To know the answer to this question today, however, one need only ask what Jesus Christ did with our transgressions and failures. Does he remind us of **them** over and over? Does he tell us he's going to **leave us** or **forsake us,** no matter how we feel about our sins? In Matthew, Chapter 18, Peter asked Jesus how many times he should forgive another person.

Matthew 18:21-22
"seven times? Jesus saith unto him, I say not unto thee, Until seven times: but, Until seventy times seven."

Again in Matthew, Chapter 6, Jesus said:

Matthew 6:14-15
*"For if ye **forgive men** their trespasses, your heavenly Father will also forgive you: But if ye **forgive not men** their trespasses, **neither** will your Father forgive your trespasses."*

You might say, "God, that's not fair! I have been faithful to my partner, and he/she was unfaithful to me." Could not the Lord say the same of you and me, in our unfaithfulness to Him? We must see that God's method of bookkeeping is unique. If your husband or wife has been unfaithful to you, and you've been the husband or wife God tells you you should be, then **that sin is on your spouse's record**, and your record is unblemished. This is made clear in the book of Hebrews.

243

Hebrews 13:4

"Marriage is honorable in all, and the bed undefiled: but whoremongers and adulterers God will judge."

If your husband or wife is unfaithful to you, and you **do not forgive**; if you allow bitterness, hurt, resentment, hatred, or retaliation to lodge in your heart, **that is on your record**, and you will suffer for it also. Just remember, you do not have to get revenge. Just completely forgive him or her in Jesus' name, and let God do as He sees fit.

I have known of instances, where partners have committed an act of adultery in a weak moment, only to repent completely and see healing and future fruitfulness come, following that dark moment. I have seen other situations, where wives have known of their husband's infidelity, and have forgiven them, loved them, and cared for them as though it were not happening. These women knew how to *"cast all their care on him, for he cares for you* (them)." (I Peter 5:7) I watched, as years went by, and infidelity went on. Did God not see? Oh yes! I have watched, and seen these same unrepentant adulterers come to a horrible end. The forgiving partner, was then *"loosed"* by God, and his/her disposition manifested a beautiful Christ-likeness, because of the years of having to trust Christ for strength each day.

In contrast, I've seen other "innocent partners" become immersed in self-pity and complaining. I've seen a sweet disposition, become hard and untrusting. One can almost watch as these poor people dig their own graves. By allowing themselves the "privilege" of unforgiveness and resentment, they begin to deteriorate from within, and lose the peace of knowing their sins are forgiven. In Matthew 18:21-35, and in Matthew, Chapter 6, Jesus describes the price one pays for failure to forgive others.

Matthew 6:15

"But if ye forgive not men their trespasses, neither will your Father forgive your trespasses."

As soon as I quote this verse, I hear some say, "Oh, I've forgiven my former partner completely." Have you? Are you loving them, and showing affection to them, as you did before the offense? If not, you've only agreed to detente. You've forgiven, but want nothing more to do with them—you don't want them around. Let me say to you, **that isn't forgiveness,** as **the word of God** speaks of forgiveness. Paul the Apostle, said in Ephesians, Chapter 4, our forgiveness must be Christ like.

Ephesians 4:32

"...forgiving one another, even as God for Christ's sake hath forgiven you."

"Even as!" This speaks not only of the **deed of forgiveness,** but the **degree of forgiveness. Completely!** Most persons, have "buried the hatchet" with the handle sticking out of the ground. This makes it convenient to pull it out again later, to use as an excuse for their unchristlike attitudes and actions. When Christ forgives, He **forgives** completely, **forgets** completely, **restores** completely, **loves** completely, and **never separates** from us, or **reminds** us of our past—**if we repent of our sins.**

Remember now, the Word says that we may *"live separately,"* but that **does not grant permission to marry a second spouse, or to harbor resentment, bitterness, hatred, or retaliation in our hearts, under any circumstances.**

QUESTION

How can anyone possibly have a continuing love relationship with their marriage partner after that partner has committed adultery with another person?

ANSWER

Jesus gives us **three levels** at which we may love those who have wronged us:

☞   *"Husbands love your wives."*
☞   *"Love thy neighbor as thyself."*
☞   *"Love your enemies."*

Jesus simply commanded us to **love others**. You will have to **choose the level** at which you will love others, every day of your life. If you **truly love** Jesus Christ, **you will love**. I John Chapter 3 speaks very clearly of this.

I John 4:7-8
*"Beloved, let us love one another: for love is of God; and every one that loveth is born of God, and knoweth God. He that **loveth not knoweth not God**; for God is love."*

Note: If you **cannot love completely,** you have not **forgiven completely,** *"Even as God for Christ's sake hath forgiven you:"*

QUESTION

I don't care what you say, I have divorced and married a second time, and feel no condemnation whatsoever!

ANSWER

Our **feelings,** have **nothing whatsoever** to do with truth and error. Nowhere does it say we'll be judged by our **feelings,** or by what **we think. We will be judged by what the Word of God declares.**

Many times in my ministry I've had unsaved people say, "Preacher, I just want you to know, I feel no fear of dying whatsoever."

"Do you mean you're not afraid of the grave?"

"Not a bit!"

"That's something! Did you know the Bible says that death and the grave are not the end?"

"What do you mean?"

"The Bible says that **death is a door**, and we decide in this lifew where we'll spend eternity."

"Really?"

"Really!"

Hebrews 9:27

"And as it is appointed unto men once to die, but after this the judgment:"

He said, "I didn't know that!"

"I didn't think so," I replied.

Suddenly, the Holy Spirit brings to these souls truth they had never seen before, and their concept of death, takes on a totally different perspective.

I wouldn't want anyone to feel condemned by anything I have said. If the Holy Spirit shows you that what I've said is consistent with the eternal Word of God (by which we shall be judged), then, regardless of our feelings, we must act in obedience to that Word. Once Bible truth has gotten inside of you, you will never again have genuine peace, until you act upon that truth.

QUESTION

I know of a sweet couple in our church that have three children. Both the man and woman were divorced before they married each other. Are you saying that God wants to break up that sweet Christian home, and leave those children destitute?

ANSWER

Let me repeat, **I am not saying what anyone should do**. I am only telling you what the Word of God says. If you want to argue with the Word of God, that's your prerogative. It makes no difference how nice, or how sweet, or how religious any person or couple might be. If they come under the Bible description of **"whosoever,"** as it is found, in Mark 10:11 and Luke 16:18, then this truth applies.

First, you stated that this couple were both previously married, divorced, and have now become married to each other. Never mind what I say about them, **Jesus said they are** *"adulterers"* in Matthew, Chapters 5, and 19, Mark, Chapter 10, Luke, Chapter 16, and Paul, in Romans 7:2-3 all said we should call them adulterers and adulteresses, unless their first partners have died, and then warned us *"be not deceived"* about this. I Corinthians, Chapter 6 states:

I Corinthians 6:9-10
"Be not deceived: neither fornicators...nor adulterers...shall inherit the kingdom of God."

If Jesus and Paul said, that that "sweet couple's" present relationship is **an adulterous one**, and children born into that adulterous relationship are **illegitimate**, theirs may be a **religious home,** but **not a sweet Christian home**.

Now, if what Jesus and Paul said is true, that this couple is and will be **lost for eternity,** unless they repent of their

248

adulterous relationship, what would you recommend that they do?

Until this couple sees their lost condition, according to the Word of God, and forget what many modern day authors say, they will **never turn**. You may think that this would be a cruel message to bring to them, but if no one tells them of their lost condition, how will they ever know before it is too late? I believe it's more merciful to warn them of this truth, than to let them **die in their sins, thinking they're going to heaven**.

If this couple, were to sit down with the children and explain to them the **seriousness of this sin in God's sight**, and let them know **the cost of repentance**, the children would then have a vivid example of **the cost, of disobedience to God's Word**. The action of the parents, could **break the spirit** of divorce and adultery in the family, and the children might be saved from the same fate.

I wonder how this **"Christian couple"** would explain to their **original partners and children,** that this **new relationship** (illegitimate in God's sight), was ordered by God, and that **their original relationships,** were now no longer valid. If they could show the validity of the second (illegitimate) relationship, what would prevent them from justifying a third, fourth, or fifth relationship?

To assume that this couple is "Christian" because they **look** or **act** like it, is to **deny the Word**. Thus, **if according to the Scripture**, they are **adulterers**, then **they are not Christians,** and **their home is not Christian, or legal,** in God's eyes. When these individuals divorced the first time, violating a life-long covenant, and then married another person, while their first spouse was still living, they demonstrated several things.

☞ They possessed an unforgiving spirit.

☞ They never intended to forgive as Christ forgives, nor to continue to love the one, to whom they originally pledged their life.

249

☞ They have now moved into a position (married again), which, in the natural, makes reconciliation virtually impossible in the future.

In Matthew, Christ's assessment of **genuine forgiveness,** is very plain.

Matthew 6:15
"But if ye forgive not men their trespasses, neither will your Father forgive your trespasses."

Matthew 18:34-35
"And his lord was wroth, and delivered him to the tormentors, till he should pay all that was due unto him. **so likewise shall my heavenly Father do also unto you,** *if ye from your hearts forgive not every one his brother their trespasses."*

Other corresponding verses would be:
Romans 12:19
Ephesians 4:32
Colossians 3:13
I Peter 3:9.

QUESTION

My husband and I, each having married for the first time, divorced two years ago. Recently, we began seeing each other again, trying to see if we could make it work this time. During these times together we have had physical relations when he has stayed at my apartment. When I shared this with a Christian counselor, he told me I must stop this. He said, "Unless you remarry him, you are committing adultery." Is this true?

ANSWER

Your question is a good example of why the Church is in such confusion on the subject of marriage, divorce and adulterous marriages. Jesus described the Church's present-day situation well, in Matthew, Chapter 15, as it being a case of *"the blind leading the blind."* Again let me say, the **marriage license,** has **nothing** to do with your *"one flesh"* position before God. Likewise, a **divorce certificate,** does not effect the *"one flesh"* **condition** one bit.

> **Mark 10:9 (Living Bible)**
> *"No man may separate what God hath joined together."*

The judge that issued you the divorce papers, **did not** unite you, and, thus, **cannot divide you. God alone** does that, and **only at death**.

It is encouraging to see that you and your husband are trying to work it out. In I Corinthians, Chapter 7, Paul gives parameters for these circumstances.

> **I Corinthians 7:11**
> *"But and if she depart, let her **remain unmarried, or be reconciled** to her **husband."***

In God's sight, a husband and wife who are separated, have **no other choices** but these:
- ☞   Remain separated.
- ☞   Be reconciled to their spouse.

In God's sight, you and your husband are not only *"one flesh"* now, but **shall be until death parts you**. Therefore, in God's sight, physical relations in love between you and your husband are **right**. Sex is a privilege of marriage, and although adultery **violates** the covenant; it **does not dissolve it**.

My only caution would be that you be very discerning concerning your spouse's **true intentions**. Sometimes their conciliatory actions, can be a way of having their cake and eating it too. The better part of wisdom in today's society, would be to very carefully investigate the activities that your spouse may have participated in while you were apart. If there is **any possibility**, that he/she may have contracted a disease, **demand a complete medical test before you renew physical relations.** If your spouse **sincerely** wants to reconcile, and there are no medical complications, your relationship is not in any way illegal in God's eyes. I would suggest, however, that you renew your vows at the earliest possible date, to *"avoid the appearance of evil"* in your neighborhood.

Hebrews 13:4
"Marriage is honorable in all, and the bed undefiled..."

But know also that sexual relations, whether physical or mental, with **any other** than your *"one flesh"* spouse, are described in the Word of God as **adulterous**.

QUESTION

My pastor divorced and has married again. Does that mean my pastor isn't a Christian?

ANSWER

I must give a two fold answer here. First, the fact that a man is in a ministry office, has no effect on Bible truth. If a pastor, deacon, teacher, trustee, T.V. personality, or internationally-known evangelist has married, divorced and married another spouse, **while his first wife is still alive**, it matters not how **popular** he may be: According to God's Word he comes under the heading of "**whosoever**."

Luke 16:18

*"**whosoever** putteth away his wife, and marrieth another, committeth **adultery**."*

Paul reinforces this to the Church, in Romans, Chapter 7.

Romans 7:3

*"..she shall be called an **adulteress**..."*

Paul said it, I didn't.

You may say, "But this man is so gifted and talented. I've learned so much from him." Maybe you even accepted Christ through his ministry.

I know personally of men with great followings, who have seemingly had tremendous success in leading a great number of souls to Christ, and have had apparent miracles happening in their services. These are men, whose personal lives **were a moral disaster**. One I know of, had illicit relations with one or more women in every church he pastored. Another, had women lived with him in his motel rooms during revival meetings, while his family was at home. In each case, **their public ministry was incredible**.

You must understand **first**, that, in most cases, these men have **great natural ability** to sway and convince crowds. **Secondly**, if they preach Scripture, God will honor His Word with fruit. It doesn't make any difference how gifted a man may be. The magicians in Egypt, performed the same miracles as Moses, yet were empowered by Satan (Matthew 7:10-12). In Matthew, Jesus spoke of signs in the last days.

Matthew 24:24:

*"For there shall arise false Christs, and false prophets, and shall shew great signs and wonders; insomuch that, if it were possible, **they shall deceive the very elect.**"*

Matthew 7:21-23

*"Not every one that saith unto me, Lord, Lord, shall enter into the kingdom of heaven; but he that **doeth** the will of My Father which is in heaven. Many will say to me in that day, Lord, Lord, have we not prophesied in thy name? and in thy name have cast out devils? And in thy name done **many wonderful works?** And then will I profess unto them, I never new you: depart from me, ye that work iniquity* (or lawlessness).*"*

I know that I am walking on the sacred ground of many pet doctrines, and kicking over some very sacred cows. **I also realize** there will be many who won't enjoy hearing this, but it's totally consistent with all of the Word of God, and, therefore, **I dare not apologize for it.**

Many today, are following, so called "men of God," who **scripturally,** are totally disqualified to lead them into spiritual paths. Paul says, that every saint has the same responsibility **today,** as Paul placed upon the Corinthian believers of his day.

I Corinthians 11:1

*"Be ye followers of me, **even as I also am of Christ.**"*

Paul was saying, that a shepherd should be one **whose life can be imitated**. In Hebrews, Chapter 13, he made it even clearer, concerning those who have "authority over you."

Hebrews 13:7

*"Remember them which have the **rule** over you, who have spoken unto you the word of God: **whose faith follow**,* (or imitate) *considering **the end of their conversation*** (or make it a goal of your life to trust the Lord **as they do**)."

When choosing a spiritual leader, Scripture tells us that his personal and public conduct must be such, that you can use it as a model to **imitate, in every area.** This is why it behooves every saint, to read I Timothy, Chapter 3, and Titus, Chapter 1, **before submitting** to **any man's ministry.**

I Timothy 3:1-13

"This is a **true saying,** (Remember the Word of God says, *'ye shall know the **truth** and the **truth** will make you free'*) *If a man desire the office of a bishop,* (or elder, or pastor) *he desireth a good work. A bishop then must be **blameless, the husband** of one wife,* (literally 'a one-woman man') *vigilant, sober, of good behavior, given to hospitality, apt to teach; Not given to wine, no striker, not greedy of filthy lucre; but patient, not a brawler, not covetous; **one that ruleth well his own house, having his children in subjection with all gravity;*** (The Living Bible— *'who obey quickly and quietly,'*) *(For if a **man know not how to rule his own house, how shall he take care of the church of God?**) Not a novice, lest being lifted up with pride he fall into the condemnation of the devil. Moreover he must have a good report of them that are without; lest he fall into reproach and the snare of the devil."*

Verses 8-13, are concerning deacons. **Do these verses describe your shepherd?** "Well we can't judge," you may say. Then **why are these verses here?** One of the greatest problems in the churches today, is *"the blind leading the blind and all falling in ditches,"* **because of compromising the Word of God.**

These are the clear biblical standards for shepherds. If they fail to **fulfill these requirements**, a sheep **shouldn't follow them**.

This one statement which I just made, has made more pastors, evangelists, and church officers angry with **me** than any other. These men act as though I **wrote those verses**, that I'm out to hurt them. Nothing can be further from the truth. I'm only **declaring the eternal truth of God's word,** which is **clearly** stated in these verses. I am in hopes, that these men will allow it to **change their conduct**. The tendency today is to twist the **word of God,** to **excuse our conduct**, rather than to change our **conduct,** and align **it** with the **eternal word of God**.

To divorce and marry again, while our first partner is alive **does constitute adultery in God's eyes**, and shall be judged accordingly. This is true, regardless of **who** I am, **what** office I hold, or **ministry I perform**. Peter declared this very succinctly, in Acts, Chapter 10.

Acts 10:34

"Of a truth I perceive that God is no respecter of persons."

Again in Deuteronomy, Chapter 10, Moses said:

Deuteronomy 10:17

*"For the Lord your God is God of gods, and Lord of lords, a great God, a mighty, and a terrible, **which regardeth not persons, nor taketh reward.***" (Living Bible, *"and takes no bribes.")*

In Titus, Chapter 1, Paul instructed Titus how to appoint **elders** (or pastors).

Titus 1:6-9

*"If any be blameless, **the husband of one wife,** (one-woman man) **having faithful children not accused of riot or**

256

unruly. For a bishop must be blameless, as the steward of God; not self-willed, not soon angry, not given to wine, no striker, not given to filthy lucre; But a lover of hospitality, a lover of good men, sober, just, holy, temperate; **Holding fast the faithful word** *as he hath been taught, that he may be able by* **sound doctrine** *(example and precept together)* **both to exhort** *(teach)* **and to convince** *(by example)* **the gainsayers.** *(verse 10 goes on)* **For there are many unruly and vain talkers and deceivers..."**

You will notice, that **none** of **the manifestation gifts,** which Paul described in I Corinthians, Chapter 12, are named in these verses. Instead, there are **clear definitions of righteous character.** No matter how gifted the man may be, how sweet, how loving, or **anointed;** if he doesn't line up with these portions in Timothy and Titus, Paul says, **he is not scripturally qualified** to shepherd or pastor a flock. These are the **minimum requirements!**

I didn't say it, Paul did, under the inspiration of the Spirit of God. It is contained in a book, that is *"settled forever in the heavens"* (Psalms 118:89); and is *"like silver, seven times refined."* It is the same word that will judge us (John 12:48) in the end.

I know there are many efforts today to try to explain these truths away. These efforts will not succeed, however, for **God said it, and thus it stands.** We may choose not to obey it; but in disobeying, we are *"sowing to the wind, and will reap the whirlwind, (Hosea 8:7) sowing to the flesh, and will reap corruption (Galatians 6:8)."*

How I pray, that the **true church** of Jesus Christ will awaken before it's too late; that the **"elect,"** will not be deceived. I know we're being told that we are living in a new age of enlightenment, no longer bound by the obsolete victorian standards of morality. **Rubbish!** Our society's new lifestyle, and man's so-called new morality, **does not change God's eternal**

257

standards of righteousness and morality one iota, as they are revealed in His Word, The Holy Bible! David the Psalmist said it well.

> **Psalms 119:89**
> *"For ever, O Lord, thy word is **settled in heaven**."*

QUESTION

How can a pastor of a church ever preach this message in the day in which we live?

ANSWER

No pastor should ever preach this message anywhere until:

- ☞ **It has become a deep-seated conviction** within him.

- ☞ **He knows with a certainty** that he is in the ministry **because he is called of God** to preach the Word, and not to tickle men's ears.

- ☞ **He knows this message is consistent** with the whole Bible. Knowing this, he will then have to quit trying to adjust this message to his theology, and instead, adjust his theology to the Word of God.

- ☞ **He knows he is called of God** and **not hired by the church**. He must believe that **God is his source,** and **not the church**. By that I mean, he will have to say, **"I'll preach it even if I lose my church, parsonage, retirement fund, and denominational affiliation and/or ordination. God is my source!** If I'm faithful to the Word, He'll be faithful to me."

- ☞ **You are no longer concerned about what your church might do to you,** if you preach something they don't like. Instead, **fear God,** lest you compromise

His Word. Until then, you **never will,** or **never should** preach it. Proverbs, Chapter 29, tells why.

Proverbs 29:25
"The fear of man bringeth a snare..."

☞ **He knows that anytime he stands for God's Word, whatever he loses, the Lord will repay him** one hundred times over in this life (Mark 10:29-30). **If you cannot believe this, don't preach it.**

I have seen God perform miracles in providing abundantly for me throughout my ministry, during recession, inflation, etc., because **He is my source.**

QUESTION

For some of us this truth has come too late, since I am divorced and have already married another spouse. I know it is truth, but how should one respond?

ANSWER

To start with, let me say that it is the devil's job to cause feelings of discouragement, hopelessness, desperation, and anger. He likes to cause people to make rash, forced decisions, for which they later must pay dearly. He tells them that they must **act now!**

The work of the Holy Spirit is not like this. His purpose is to reveal sin that must be dealt with, that a person might have abundant life. He will convict only for the purpose of showing you God's divine standard, and encouraging you to desire that standard in your life. The Holy Spirit does not condemn, punish, or reject you. The very fact that He shows us our sin, is evidence of God's great love for us.

Therefore, if, upon hearing this message, you feel condemned, hopeless, helpless, or compelled to act rashly, **know that that is not how God operates**.

I would encourage you to use these guidelines as you apply this truth.

☞ **As an act of your will**, place **the consequences of this truth** you've learned aside for a few moments. By that I mean, **those thoughts** that say, "If this is true, then that means I **must do this** or **that**, or leave him/her, etc."

☞ Let the Holy Spirit tell you whether this message is true or not. Let it become a deep conviction in your heart, **based solely upon the Word of God**. If you just keep asking more people what they **think**, you will end up in confusion.

☞ **Repent** of the area of sin the Holy Spirit has revealed to you, by agreeing with God that it **is sin**. If the sin is adultery, **verbalize it**. "**I have committed adultery**, and violated my vow before You. **I recognize** that is sin, and I don't want that sin, or any other sins related to adultery in my life. **I renounce** this sin in the name of Jesus, and ask that you forgive me and cleanse me with the precious blood of Jesus. Thank you for forgiving me...in Jesus' name."

☞ Forgive **yourself completely**. Know that God loves you very much, and revealed these things to you as proof of His love. He already suffered for your sin, so you wouldn't have to.

☞ **Resolve before the Lord,** that you will do **whatever is necessary** to be in a right relationship with Him; but you will do **nothing,** until the Holy Spirit directs you to. When the Holy Spirit directs you to do something, it will not be a **desperate act,** born out of fear of divine judgment. It will instead, be **a deliberate act,** born out of a deep-seated conviction, and peace, that

260

"this is the will of God concerning me,"—**Not an act of self-pity**, but rather of **spiritual expectation and confidence** in God's Word. Remember what Jesus said, in Mark, Chapter 10.

Mark 10:28-30

*"Then Peter began to say unto him, Lo, we have left all, and have followed thee. And Jesus answered and said, Verily I say unto you, **there is no man** that hath left house, or brethren, or sisters, or father, or mother, or wife, or children, or lands, for my sake, and the gospel's, But he shall receive an hundredfold now in this time, houses, and brethren, and sisters, and mothers, and children, and lands, **with persecutions; and in the world to come eternal life."***

No one else can tell you how the Holy Spirit will direct you as you acknowledge this message. **It will always be consistent with the Word of God,** but uniquely patterned for you. Some have said, "Jesus is all I need," and have directed all their energies toward ministering to others. Some have seen the Lord ever so slowly **resolve** old irreconcilable circumstances, **rekindle** mutual respect and admiration, and **initiate** reunion. Others, are presently joyfully and peacefully, functioning in a separated platonic relationship, while caring for the children, and unashamedly thanking the Lord for the **release and spiritual freedom** Christ has brought into their lives.

I cannot tell you how the Holy Spirit will direct you. However it is, and it may be hard, it will be with a deep inward peace and conviction, that *"This is the will of God in Christ Jesus concerning me."*

If this generation continues on its present course, disaster and judgment are sure. Homes are disintegrating, and no church is any stronger than the composite strength of each individual home. If the family is weak, the home is weak. If the churches are spiritually weak, it's because we have **rationalized or disregarded scriptural principles somewhere along the way. I refuse to blame God for our weakness and disarray.** It is Christ's Church that has forsaken God's standard, with the resultant chaos, that has left society with no example to follow.

If that same church will (since *"judgment must begin at the house of God"* I Peter 4:17) submit to, and obey these standards in God's Word concerning morality, they will elevate the Church's standards and morality, to a place where that church and society itself, will experience an inward release of freedom, **unknown to them before this time.** I know the world says that **morality restricts,** but the Lord Jesus Christ said just the opposite.

John 8:32
   *"and ye shall know the **truth**, and the **truth** shall make you free."*

Divine absolutes, were not given to restrict mankind and make him miserable, but to free and protect him.

Special Note
Whenever divine absolutes are removed from national or personal life, corruption, confusion, weakness and decay set in.

Many of you know that if someone had tried to legalize or popularize adultery, illicit sex, dope, or sodomy in the true Church sixty or seventy years ago, they would have been run out of town. Shouldn't the very fact that it's happening publicly with hardly an outcry of protest tell us something? Does it indicate that the Church is closer, or further away from God's standard? **Further!**

I know that some people feel that this truth seems to be coming too late for them. Thank God, it's still in time for the next generation. **Our youth today are looking for absolutes**. They are being told there are none. **May God help the true people of God, to sound the cry, that His standards are absolute.**

I know that this book will not answer all your questions; but if you will study it deeply, it will cause you to know **God's truth** concerning all marriages. They are **universally** and **divinely** formed by God, **through the vows of the participants**. **They are sealed, regardless of your or my behavior, "till death do us part."**

AMEN

If this book has been a help or blessing to you and you would like to receive additional information concerning other taped messages by Joseph Webb, write your request to:

Webb Ministries Inc.
P. O. Box 520729
Longwood, FL 32752-0729

Additional Christian Teaching available...

Books:

How To Train Up A Child - $4.95

This 30 page book presents sound, clear biblical principles for "Training up" godly children who will "rise up and call you blessed". This author has, by experience, found a sound formula in God's Word which, if used consistently, will succeed for you.

This is a significant step-by-step guide for every parent, grandparent, or teacher who wishes to experience greater success in raising godly children.

Once you discover the biblical family principles of discipline and begin to practice them as they are disclosed and demonstrated in this book, you will begin to sense that our task, although awesome, will produce long term results that will prove to be very much worth the effort! We must realize that our children are the only earthly possession we can take with us to heaven.

Trojan Horse Within the Church - $1.50

A most phenomenal 14 page pamphlet providing intriguing insights into the invasion of today's Church by the Prince of Humanist and designed as an introductory work, stimulating further study on what the Bible has to say about marriage. This pamphlet is designed to be sent to teachers, leaders and pastors.

Tapes:

Marriage, Divorce and New Relationships - 5 Tape Series   **$18.00**
     A one-day seminar on this critical subject, presented by Joseph Webb. These tapes include truths and explanations of previously unclear and seemingly contradictory verses; plus answers to many question asked by those in attendance.

The Renewing of the Mind - 4 Tape Series   **$13.00**
     Have you ever wondered if Christians could have continuous victory in their daily thought life? Here is a clear scriptural presentation of how it is possible, with simple but effective steps to make it a reality in your daily life. Many have said this series has changed their lives.

Recognizing a True Christian - 6 Tape Series   **$19.00**
     This series of tapes brings together, in a balanced way, the New Testament evidences of a genuine, *born again* believer. They will help you to discern between *wheat and tares*, and minister more effectively in your soul winning efforts.

What Love Really Is - 2 Tape Series   **$7.00**
     This is one of the most electrifying teachings I have ever heard on the meaning of *scriptural love* taught by Joseph Webb's son, Jeff. It will help you to grasp what New Testament love really means, and help you to see I Corinthians 13 in an entirely different light.

Biblical Principles for Christian Families - 15 Tapes Series   **$50.00**

This series of tapes is a clear and comprehensive study of pertinent Biblical principles regarding courting, engagement, marriage, starting a family, rearing a family, interpersonal relationships within a family, parenting and grandparenting.

This series of messages is the end result of over thirty-five years of study and counselling experience by Joseph Webb. Every Christian family should make this set a mandatory study guide for young and old in their home.

Comments From Listeners of This Series

"I will not marry my future partner until they hear this set of tapes."

"I only wish I had known these principles when I was younger...what a difference it could have made in my home!"

"It is much easier to take a stand in my home when I know I am being obedient to the Lord."

"This is scriptural dynamite."

You and Your Money - 5 tape series (minimum donation) **$20**

This series teaches that all our possessions are a trust from God and must be earned and managed according to scriptural principles if we are to expect God's blessings. It is filled with examples of how to apply these principles. When I first learned this truth I was deeply in debt and by applying them God has brought me out of the pit of debt. They will work for you.

Sowing and Reaping - 5 tape series (minimum donation) **$20**

This series explains a universal law that applies in every area of our lives, and always works. The application in this series is related to the importance of witnessing for Christ, with it's attendant benefits both now and in eternity. It will challenge you to plant your seeds.

Useable Vessels - 8 tape series (minimum donation) **$32**

What are the four qualities that must be developed in a believer if he is to be profitably used by God? Once you learn and apply them it will revolutionize your life.

Good Things for God's People - 20 tape series (min. donation) **$88**

The Bible lists five major things that are good for believers. Many believers complain when things happen to them, because they don't recognize their eternal benefits. If you learn to recognize them when they come, they will bring you confidence, joy and maturity.

The Tongue - 12 tape series (minimum donation) **$45**

This is not a "name it and claim it" message, but an in depth study of the everyday struggle of a believer as he encounters the worldly influence of his society, and the scriptural basis for overcoming it. It defines the enemies ploys and the biblical means of becoming an overcomer. It describes the ongoing war, and the promised means of victory, in clear practical language. The last part of this series gives six basic biblical conclusions concerning our tongue. If you desire to mature quickly, this set is a must!

Scriptural Standards for a Pastor - 3 tapes (min. donation) **$15.00**

These tapes contain an in depth study of the biblical requirements for one called to be a pastor. Many pastors will never teach on this subject because of fear or embarrassment, but the word of God is very clear and must be understood by any believers today who are looking for a biblically qualified shepherd.

Note: All prices on books and tapes are subject to change without notice.

Order Form

Quan.	Books	Minimum Donation
_____	Till Death Do Us Part?	$12.95
_____	How to Train Up a Child	$4.95
_____	Trojan Horse Within the Church	$1.50

Quan.	Audio Tapes	
_____	Marriage and Divorce Seminar	$18.00
_____	Renewing of the Mind	$13.00
_____	Recognizing a True Christian	$19.00
_____	What Love Really Is	$ 7.00
_____	Biblical Prin. for Chr. Fam.	$50.00

Quan.	New Tapes	
_____	You and Your Money	$20.00
_____	Sowing and Reaping	$20.00
_____	Useable Vessels	$32.00
_____	Good Things for God's People	$88.00
_____	The Tongue	$45.00
_____	Scriptural Standards for a Pastor	$15.00

$_____ Subtotal

$ 2.50_____ Postage/Handling for first two books

$_____ NOTE: Please add $1.00 extra for each
additional 2 books

$_____ Total Enclosed (U.S. Dollars Only)

Name_____

Street_____

City _____ State_____ ZIP_____

"*Son of dust he said, I'm sending you ... to a nation rebelling against me. They and their fathers have kept on sinning against me until this very hour. For they are a hardhearted, stiffnecked people. But I am sending you to give them my messages —The messages of the Lord God. And whether they listen or not (for remember, they are rebels), they will at least know they had a prophet among them.*

Son of dust, don't be afraid of them; don't be frightened even though their threats are sharp and barbed and sting like scorpions, Don't be dismayed by their dark scowls. For remember, They are rebels!

You must give them my messages whether they listen or not."

Ezekiel 2:3-7
The Living Bible

Index

273